To: Sandra
an awesome eff[...]
ChristLike Worker.
God Bless

D0328993

How to Become Wealthy While Young!

80
Proven Ways
to become
A Millionaire

All you need is two or three!

by
Paul S. Damazo

SG&A Productions, Inc.

Published by SG&A Productions, Inc., San Rafael, CA USA
www.80ProvenWaysToBecomeAMillionaire.com
800-310-5389

This book is designed to inspire you into action and to provide accurate and authoritative information in regard to the subject matter covered. Factual material has been obtained from sources believed to be reliable, and is not guaranteed. All examples are for illustrative purposes only and are not to be construed as recommendations, advice, or tax counsel. The author and publisher are not engaged in rendering legal, accounting, or other professional service. If legal or other expert assistance is required, the author and publisher strongly recommend that the reader should contact his own professional advisors.

ISBN: 978-0-9793139-8-1
Library of Congress Control Number: 2007926605

Printed in the United States of America

Book Design: Renée Robinson of SG&A Productions, Inc.
Editor: Clifford Goldstein
Copy Editor: John Maybury of goofbuster.com
Author Portrait: Wilmer Snyder

Book is available at special quantity discounts to use for gifts, sales promotions, employee or client premiums, churches, fundraising organizations, or educational purposes.

Table of Contents

What Others Have to Say

This is a powerful text that outlines Paul's proven methods of becoming a winner in a rough and tumble economy, not a get-rich-quick manual.

DR. ROLAND J. HILL
Author, *Wealth Without Guilt*
#1 Theo-Economist in the U.S.

Paul Damazo brings an incredible "wealth" of experience to the topic he has written about. You can just feel his selfless passion to help others learn their way to financial independence. What he said makes so much sense. I've learned so much.

CLIFFORD GOLDSTEIN
Writer, editor, author of 18 books

I found a better way to get my finances under control and grow wealth by following Paul Damazo's road map to becoming a millionaire with 80 different ways to get there. It's working and the benefits are huge!

DAWN HIBBARD
Station Manager, 89.7 FM KSGN

My two teenage daughters were so excited after one of his seminars, they asked us to invest their allowances and birthday money as Mr. Damazo suggested and now they are actively watching their money compound.

LARRY D. McGILL, PH.D., J.D.
Pastor/Attorney/Marriage Counselor

In his typical enthusiastic and confident way, Paul Damazo provides insight and understanding into what is a mystery for many—how personal finance works. Whether you are young or old, this book provides financial information that can provide valuable guidance as you plan for your financial future.

DON VAN ORNAM, PH.D.
Dean, School of Business
Southern University

This book enables the reader to make informed decisions about their financial futures. The strategies that the author includes provide many great choices and opportunities that may enrich their lives financially. I just wish this book had been available as I started my financial life 50 years ago.

CLIFFORD W. OLSON, PH.D.
Professor of Business Administration,
Southern University

It takes a wise person to learn from the experience of others; any fool can learn from his own—and you don't have time in today's economic environment to experiment. Learn from an expert! Provide for your family and then enjoy giving away your millions to make the world a better place!

LAWRENCE T. GERATY, PH.D.
President, La Sierra University

Why This Book?

The author has a passion for you to live a far better financial, joyous life with time to smell the roses along the way. This book will be a gigantic help to all ages—regardless if you are single, married, divorced, and are a parent or not.

This book covers finances from the womb to the tomb, and offers significant financial solutions and options. It will teach you how to take charge of your own financial future.

You will learn:

$ How to be like Arkad, the richest man in old Babylon, who was rich, generous, and each year his wealth increased faster than he spent it.

$ How your children can be worth $15 million by age 45 so they can retire wealthy while young.

$ How to use your home to make you a millionaire, whether it's paid for or not.

$ How to earn an average annual return of 15% on all your investments   if the author can do it for 50 years, so can you.

$ How to leave college debt-free without the help of your parents, and have more than $300,000 invested by graduation.

$ 80 proven ways to become a millionaire—you need only two or three.

$ Two simple investments that will pay you 100% per year for life.

$ How newlyweds can be worth $10 million 20 years from their wedding day.

$ How to become a millionaire, even if you're starting late!

$ How to have your money work hard for you, rather than you working hard for your money!

$ How to have multiple streams of ongoing income, even in retirement.

This book can change your financial life now, and for the rest of your life. It can also change the financial life of your children and granchildren.

If every person could get out of debt, save and invest for themselves, and make the choice to be rich, their lives would change significantly.

There would be a snowball effect that would also change this country. There would be more savings, which would create more jobs. The government would be able to spend less on taking care of people, which would mean lower taxes, which would mean more money in your pocket.

*Wealth is not a matter of chance,
it's a matter of choice—your choice!*

Dedication

This book is dedicated to my dear friend and colleague Heather Miller, SIFE Faculty Fellow and Director of Special Projects, School of Business, and to the Students In Free Enterprise (SIFE) team at La Sierra University, Riverside, California. For many years SIFE has helped me bring this important message to the community in Riverside and other places.

Thank you, Heather, you and your colleagues have inspired those magnificent students to learn the principles of wealth creation, and helped them translate the ideas into lessons for thousands of children and youth. The enthusiasm, selflessness, and teachable spirit of all of the SIFE members and leaders is a shining example.

About SIFE Worldwide

Students In Free Enterprise (SIFE) is an international organization of college students who make a difference in their communities through free-enterprise projects. SIFE was started by corporate America in 1975 as a way to offer college students the opportunity to develop leadership, teamwork, and communication skills through learning, practicing, and teaching the principles of free enterprise and the entrepreneurial spirit.

La Sierra University is one of almost 2,000 universities in more than 40 countries that sponsor a SIFE team. Congratulations to La Sierra University and the SIFE' team and Heather Miller.

- For being the international champions four times
- For winning the World Cup award
- For winning more than 100 trophies in special competitions

Thank you for being number one in my heart and the world.

Acknowledgments

I would like to thank the following individuals for their major respective contributions that made this book a reality.

Nancy Bender, for her numerous hours entering all the data into the computer, preliminary editing, and her recognition of the importance of this book. Many times she sacrificed her schedule to accommodate mine.

Jay Damazo, my dear wife, for her understanding during the months of research and writing. And for keeping all types of interruptions to a minimum during the time of heavy concentration.

Dr. Clifford Goldstein, for his highly professional job of editing and quality advice.

John Maybury, for his professional job of copyediting and quick turnaround (see goofbusters.com).

Dr. George Ogum, for his financial review.

Russ Potter, a longtime, dear friend who encouraged me to write this book. He got me to follow my dream to help tens of thousands of people enjoy a better financial life by expanding my influence.

Renée Robinson, my associate, for her genius in so many areas and the major contributor for the quality and success of this book. Much appreciation for all her hard work in layout, design, final title, graphics, cover design, computer genius, and a host of other areas of expertise and contribution, a special heartfelt thanks.

Foreward

Now and then, this world hears of a person who, coming out of nowhere, becomes a financial whiz. Without family connections, without a sizzling patent that provides a hefty royalty check, and without marrying into a wealthy family, these extraordinary men and women blaze a trail for thousands to safely follow. Nothing secretive, nothing based on being in the right place at the right time—these remarkable people simply followed tried and true principles that anybody could practice.

Such has been the life of Paul S. Damazo, B.S., M.S., R.D., R.I.E. It has been my privilege to know Paul since our college years. Even in his teens, he was going full bore, juggling classes, work, and his various business enterprises. He had neither government loans nor family support; his immigrant parents were busy raising seven boys and three girls—each of them going on to college and professional schools.

Paul was soon a consultant to many schools and hospitals as they upgraded their kitchens or built new facilities. On the side, and he has many sides, he created many school industries where students lived on campus. Many of these students, either high school or college, would never have finished their academic careers without Paul's various industries, where they earned money and learned skills that became a part of their lives forever. And most often, Paul turned these industries over to those lucky schools!

Soon Paul discovered that he had to master the art of investing to increase and preserve his growing assets. Through these exciting years, he did not choose to amass a huge bank account. His acute sense of gratitude since his earliest years kept him sensitive to "give back" to others who could use a helping hand. And give he did, huge donations, always choosing where his gifts would do the most good.

He has traveled far and near, sharing the wisdom that made him what he is today. His videos and public seminars have become a fresh start for hundreds of thousands, emphasizing that it is never too late to practice at least some of his proved principles. Paul has shown us all how to live a disciplined personal life as well as follow a disciplined financial plan that works wherever tried.

This book is worth far more than its cost. It could be the beginning of a new morning for each reader.

Herbert Edgar Douglass, Th.D.
President of two colleges, associate editor of a worldwide journal, and author of 20 books

Chapter 1 | *Wealth Is a Matter of Choice—Yours Alone*

A Word About Love and Money

I'm writing this book to significantly enhance your life. Even your love life! And this single page may be the most important one of the entire book.

Money can bring you a lot, and the most important thing it can never buy. You can't buy love. You can buy a lot of imitations—but never the real thing! So don't waste money, years, or even moments trying.

Know this: Real love is always based on admiration, trust, and respect. And people especially respect others who have demonstrated the ability to manage themselves and their money. Those traits always attract quality admirers, including the kind of person who can significantly contribute to a lifetime of wise and mutual wealth management.

Conversely, the lack of money management skills in life can ruin relationships, even great relationships based on genuine love. That's because mismanaging money and wasting resources—real and potential—show a lack of respect for the relationship! More marriages are ruined by money mismanagement and financial misunderstanding than by any other factor!

So don't try to buy love. And don't let a love relationship be devastated by a lack of money management skills! The goal of this book is to bring you financial fulfillment in life plus a life worth living.

First, I want to give you a wake-up call. Then, throughout the book, significant financial solutions and options will be provided. Choose the ones that are best for you and your family. May you be inspired into action. Become excited about the possibilities. Where there is joy and happiness, abundance will follow. Many blessings as you create your enhanced financial life—and love life.

Major Obstacles to Financial Success

Remember, even with great financial intentions, you may encounter financial obstacles. Be aware so that you can choose differently.

- 80% of Americans have not had even one hour of financial education.
- 75% of all households grovel from one paycheck to the next and are just 90 days from a major financial disaster or bankruptcy, and this happens all their life.
- 70% of all households go through life in debt, needlessly.
- Only 4% of all individuals are financially ready for retirement. The other 96% go into retirement financially unprepared. The reason, according to the IRS, is instant gratification.
- 80% of success in life is determined on whom you marry. That is why you should marry the person you cannot live without, and not the person you can live with.

No Goals

Only 3% of Americans have financial goals. Consequently they have more money than the remaining 97% combined. Goals are powerful. Start with your financial goals. One possible goal could be to have financially freedom. Another could be to have your children retire by age 45 worth $10 million. I am going to show you how this can be accomplished easily.

Insufficient Time

It is simple. The earlier in life you start saving and investing, the greater your estate. Some 96% of all Americans procrastinate to save and invest for retirement, and fail to create a great life along the way.

Instant Gratification

Some time ago the IRS said 96 out of 100 Americans reach retirement age unprepared, and all because of instant gratification—not differentiating between needs and wants. Learn the difference early on and you will be a financial success.

> *"If your outgo exceeds your income,*
> *then your upkeep will be your downfall."*
> BILL CARLE

Debt

Debt robs you of your investment money while making others millionaires. Read Chapter 8 on becoming debt-free quickly.

Interest Charges

Most families pay almost $11,000 interest a year, thus robbing them of money to invest. Avoid, like the plague, paying credit card interest. See Chapter 7 for additional information and help.

Taxes

The average American pays $750,000 income tax in 40 years. Study Chapter 13 in this book to reduce income taxes legally so that you will have your money to invest for yourself.

Having Children

Not every couple needs children to be happy and fulfilled. The hardest job in America is rearing children. In addition, the cost to bring up a boy from conception to age 18 is $485,000 and for a girl an additional $35,000. This does not include college costs.

Most parents revert to day care centers to rear their children because both of them work. The largest long-term study ever conducted on this subject was recently completed by the U.S. National Institutes of Health. This study points out that the best place for any child is at home with the mother.

- Only 14% of children spend the first three years in full-time care of their parents.
- Today 16 million children are in day care centers, newborn to 4 years old. The results are children who are three times more aggressive, disobedient, defiant, combative, restless, and likely to become bullies.

Having Dependent Children

Giving children everything they want disables them for life, while ruining the parents financially. If parents enjoyed the good life with each other, as young as possible, and were then prepared for an easy retirement—that would provide a great example! Instead, a lot of people work until they die because they did not teach their children to be independent at an early age.

> *"A very rich person should leave his kids enough to do anything but not enough to do nothing."*
> WARREN BUFFETT

Learn Early in Life

$ Learn from the past, then you won't repeat it

$ Learn from your parents—why make the same mistakes that they did

$ Get an education—learn early

$ Learn from successful people

$ Attend seminars—many are free

$ Read autobiographies of successful people

$ Observe other families

$ Read financial publications

$ Learn early in life, you don't have to be old to be wise

> When we teach our children early to be financially independent they will stand on our shoulders and go further than we did.
> My parents improved over their parents.
> I have improved over my parents.
> My children have improved over my wife and me.
> That is the way it should be.

Formula for Financial Success

Financial Goals
Time
Systematic Investing
Minimize Income Tax
Diversification
Good Return
Leverage
Compound
Risk Management
Own—Don't Loan
Professional Management
Eliminate Death Taxes

You Can Succeed Financially

It boils down to one single factor. You don't start out life being wealthy; rather you build up to it as fast as you can while still enjoying life as you travel toward your goal. This book is going to help you, step by step, make it as easy as possible.

*"Experience is a wonderful thing.
It enables you to recognize a mistake
when you make it again."*

Success Stories

Here are a few stories, out of thousands, to help and encourage you along your way to becoming a multimillionaire. Much success and enjoyment!

- In 1954 Monsignor James E. McSweeney's monthly income was $25. A priest by day and a shrewd investor by night, he built up his portfolio. When he died in 1999 at age 74, his estate was nearly $1 million due to time and systematic investing.
- Herbert H. Goodman worked as a janitor all his life. He was a simple man, who worked hard. After his death, at age 90, he left $2 million to the local college and YMCA.
- Gladys Holm never made more than $15,000 a year at her job as a secretary. When she died, she left more than $18 million to a children's hospital in Chicago. How did she do it? She asked her boss how to invest, she listened, and then bought the stocks he recommended.
- Karl Hagen worked as a sign and equipment paint shop foreman. He began in the 1940s investing in stocks and continued buying them throughout his lifetime. When he died, he left a total of $3 million to Johns Hopkins University, the National Air and Space Museum, and the National Geographic Society.

The one common thread of these stories is that each person invested small amounts of money over long periods of time. Anyone can build a fortune and generate wealth. It's up to you to make it happen for yourself.

> *Wealth is not a matter of chance,*
> *it's a matter of choice—your choice.*

| Chapter 2 | *The Miracles of* *"Compounding Interest"* |

You can succeed financially! It is quite simple, boiling down to three simple secrets that go back to old Babylon. The book, *The Richest Man in Babylon,* by George S. Clason, is the most widely read book in history, after the Bible. This book shares Arkad's secrets to becoming wealthy and makes the financial concept of compound interest fun to read and easy to understand.

The story takes place in old Babylon, more than 2,600 years ago. The main character Arkad was known worldwide because of his liberality and largesse. In other words, Arkad was famous for his wealth, kindness, and generosity. He gave graciously to charities, was generous with his family, and liberal with his own expenses.

> *Arkad was rich and generous, and each year his wealth increased faster than he spent it!*

What makes his story so interesting is that Arkad did not begin life wealthy. Poor when a young man, he wanted to experience more of life than what his childhood circumstances had to offer. In the book, Arkad recounts how he observed and learned and made mistakes and gained wisdom from those mistakes. Then he shares with other characters what he has learned through a lifetime of careful study, deliberate choices, and meaningful action.

Arkad's friends were confused as to why he had so much more money than they did. As children, they had been equal. They had played, studied, and worked together. Nothing had set Arkad apart. So, what was his secret? How come Arkad had all the "luck"? Didn't they "deserve" to be wealthy?

To Arkad's childhood friends, it seemed very unfair that ordinary little Arkad somehow became the richest man in Babylon, while they struggled daily to survive.

Arkad shared with his friends that when he was younger he had obverved that many things were possible when one had wealth. Being happy and content was a great way to live and having wealth made it even easier. He consciously made the choice to be happy and wealthy! He set out to learn how to accumulate wealth and then focused on doing it well.

Arkad doesn't try to defend his good fortune or to apologize for it. Instead, he sets out to share his secrets. And what he makes very clear is that these "secrets" aren't really secret at all. **They are simple formulas anyone can learn.**

> *If you struggle to survive financially,*
> *it is because you either have failed*
> *to learn the laws that build wealth,*
> *or else you do not observe them.*

Secrets of the Richest Man in Babylon

The book boils it down to three short, simple secrets, all of which apply to you. Yes, you can become wealthy.

Secret 1

$ He found the road to wealth when he decided that **"A part of all I earn is mine to keep."**

$ He kept for himself one-tenth of all he earned to invest. I strongly recommend that you invest 15%. Start with 1% and work up to 15% or more as quickly as you can.

> *Financial freedom is a life of abundance—*
> *an abundance of*
> *money, love, great relationships, harmony, peace, and joy.*

Secret 2

$ He invested wisely.

Make your money work hard for you rather than you working hard for your money.

Arkad discovered "advice is one thing that is freely given away, and watch that you only take what is worth having." In other words, he learned that we should not believe everything we are told, or follow the advice of people who are not wise.

Have the patience and persistence to let your money grow, compounding each year.

Arkad learned to save and invest and reinvest his money. He told his friends they should put their money and that money's children (i.e., the interest or return on their money) to work for them.

Secret 3

$ **Enjoy your wealth.**

If you are serious about becoming wealthy, you will quickly differentiate between your needs versus your wants, and you will not be involved with instant gratification.

> *Arkad gave graciously to charities,*
> *was generous with his family,*
> *and each year his wealth*
> *increased faster than he could spend it.*

Little did Arkad know that more than 2,600 years ago he gave a wonderful lesson in what we know today as simple and compound interest.

Definitions

Principal	The amount of money one borrows or lends before interest is added.
Interest	Money paid for the use of someone else's money. If you borrow money or use credit, you must pay extra money to the store, lending institution, or credit card company for the privilege of using their money. In the same way, when you let a financial institution such as a bank or credit union use your money, they pay you interest for depositing your money at their institution.
Interest Rate	The price paid for using someone else's money. It is stated as a percentage of the original borrowing. It can be 6% or 50%, whatever the law allows. As an example, a 10% simple annual interest rate would mean that if you deposited $100, then at the end of one year, you would have $110 in your account.
Simple Interest	Money earned and paid to the depositor or lender.
Compound Interest	The interest paid on the original sum of money (the principal) and also the interest paid on the interest earned. The chart on the next page will help you see the value of compound interest and how it works.
Compounding	Leaving interest earned on deposit so it also earns interest.

The Amazing Effect of Compounding

Compounding can work for you or against you. When you borrow money, compounding works against you and takes more of your money, sometimes far more than the amount you initially borrowed. When you save and invest money, compounding works for you, paying you more money every day.

$10,000 Invested One Time at 15% Annually		
YEAR	SIMPLE INTEREST	COMPOUND INTEREST
5	$11,500	$20,113
10	$17,500	$40,455
15	$25,000	$81,370
20	$32,500	$163,665
25	$40,000	$329,189
30	$47,500	$662,117
35	$55,000	$1,331,755

When comparing simple and compounding interest, imagine a duck and a jet, both ready to fly. The duck takes off slowly, staying close to the ground while gradually picking up height. The jet speeds down the runway, starts climbing rapidly, eventually climbing so high and so fast it appears to be going straight up. The jet is like compounding interest.

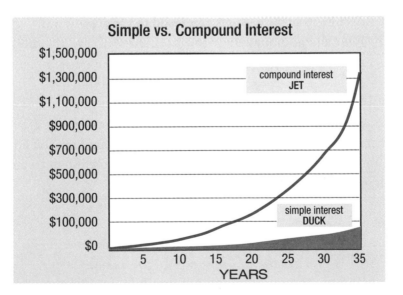

Rule of 72

Another example of compound interest is using the Rule of 72 developed by Dr. Albert Einstein, where with a 15% return your money doubles every 4.8 years. Rounding it out to five years (for simplicity's sake) you can see what a $5,000 one-time investment made at birth by parents and grandparents would amount to.

Can you imagine one's life at age 45 when the estate from a one-time investment of $5,000 has grown to $2,560,000? This awesome result is based on two major factors: compounding earned interest and time.

\$5,000 Invested One Time at 15% Compounding Annually	
YOUR AGE	AMOUNT
Birth	$5,000
5	$10,000
10	$20,000
15	$40,000
20	$80,000
25	$160,000
30	$320,000
35	$640,000
40	$1,280,000
45	$2,560,000

What I Learned from the Richest Man in Babylon

$ A part of all I earn is mine to keep.
(This is most important!)

$ Save 10%-15% of my earnings.

$ Invest the savings, using compound interest.

$ Have a large money tree. The more money I save, the more money I can put to work for me.

Food for Thought

You can become very wealthy. Compound interest grows gigantically faster than simple interest. The younger you are, the more you can use this "secret" to your advantage. Start now compounding interest and watch how fast your investments will grow.

*My assets will build up each year
faster than I can spend all the money.*

Wealthy Thinking

There are several ways to look at money.

- **Money is a pie**—when one person has more, another person has less.
  This belief results in images of lack, scarcity, and fear. This affects one's relationship with money, people, time, etc. A person who believes money is a pie usually struggles with money, relationships, and life in general.

- **Only lucky people can have money.**
  This belief keeps a person from using his or her energy and intelligence to contribute his or her own unique gifts to the world. Money is seen as a game of chance, and not as a result of a person's own intelligence and actions. People who have this belief sometimes resent others who have more money than they do. They may not realize the potential that they have to change their own life, and thus might not even try to earn or increase their money.

- **Money is bad.**
  Money is just a form of energy we use to exchange goods and services. It has no innate qualities of goodness or badness. It can be used to create more good in the world or it can be used to cause harm. The money itself is not responsible for how it is used. People choose how they will use their money. Before money was invented, people had to carry around the actual goods they were trading. People who performed work were paid in items of value such as chickens or corn or lumber or stones. Money is much more portable and versatile.

- **Money doesn't grow on trees.**
  This belief results in struggle, hard work, lack, scarcity, and fear. A person with this belief usually struggles with money, relationships, and life in general.

> *My financial freedom is created by my thoughts,
> beliefs, feelings, words, choices, and actions.*

$ **Money does grow on trees**—while you're sleeping.
This is a new belief for many. Think about it. How many
things in our daily lives come from trees? Wood for homes
and furniture, fruits such as apples and oranges, nuts, olive
oil, paper products to name a few, AND Compounding
Interest from the financial tree. This empowering way of
thinking makes a person want to plant money seeds (savings
and investments) and results in thoughts and feelings of
expansion, growth, unity, harmony, peace, and joy.

A Note About "Taking"

One of the things that Arkad learned is that people who took money
from others ended up poor, and people who gave generously tended to receive
more. At first glance, this might not seem to make sense mathematically,
until you remember that money is not a pie.

Money is a symbol that we use to exchange value. When we take
something that we did not create with our own energy, we are making a
statement that we ourselves have little value or worth. Taking from the world
through blatant stealing or more subtle manipulation reduces our value in
our own eyes and in the eyes of others. Taking reduces our worth.

As you give of your energy and talents and love to the world, you increase
your own worth, in your eyes and in the eyes of others. Contributing, and
giving back to the world in which you live, increases your life in surprising
ways. Often that increase also includes an increase in income.

Create Your Own Wealth

Wealthy thoughts, beliefs, feelings, words, and actions will help create a
life of abundance and opportunity for you. Your future, your destiny, is up
to you—not anyone else. You can begin to create options for yourself, to put
money away that will be there to finance a college education, buy a car, take
a trip to Europe, buy a house, finance any dream, or create financial freedom.
You can start building your dreams now. Your future is in your hands. What
can you do right now to find the money to invest?

A friend of mind shared that she was able to change her thoughts and
beliefs quickly after attending a *Breakthrough to Success Weekend* with Chris

Howard, one of the world's leading authorities on the psychology of wealth and accelerated personal achievement. For her it was a life-changing weekend that allowed her to break through the limitations of the past and create rapid change (see Resources). Remember, it's up to you to create your financial freedom.

You get to decide what kind of life you will have and how you can make the world a better place. You can begin right now!

> *I decide to empower myself to become wealthy!*

Time Is Magic

"Compound interest is the greatest mathematical discovery of all time," said Dr. Albert Einstein.

Results are determined by time, not just how much you invest! The next two pages give a lot of results, based on a monthly investment for different time periods. An annual rate of 15% was used because I have averaged 15% or more every year for 50 consecutive years on all my investments. I believed it, I expected it, I knew it could be achieved. And so can you!

You will see some squares shaded on the next two pages, which is summarized here. As you can see, time does make a difference!

Invested @ 15% compounded annually

	INVESTED MONTHLY	TOTAL INVESTED	PRINCIPAL/INTEREST
10 years	$100/mo	$12,000	$26,302
20 years	$50/mo	$12,000	$66,354
40 years	$25/mo	$12,000	$576,167
50 years	$20/mo	$12,000	$1,869,993

Invested @ 15% compounded annually

	INVESTED MONTHLY	TOTAL INVESTED	PRINCIPAL/INTEREST
10 years	$1,000/mo	$120,000	$263,018
20 years	$500/mo	$120,000	$663,537
25 years	$400/mo	$120,000	$1,102,625
50 years	$200/mo	$120,000	$18,699,931

Investment Results at an Annual Rate of 15%

Invest Each Month	Total $ Invested	Principal & Interest 10 yrs	Total $ Invested	Principal & Interest 15 yrs	Total $ Invested	Principal & Interest 20 yrs	Total $ Invested	Principal & Interest 25 yrs	Total $ Invested	Principal & Interest 30 yrs
$10	$1,200	$2,630	$1,800	$6,164	$2,400	$13,271	$3,000	$27,566	$3,600	$56,318
$15	$1,800	$3,945	$2,700	$9,245	$3,600	$19,906	$4,500	$41,348	$5,400	$84,477
$20	$2,400	$5,260	$3,600	$12,327	$4,800	$26,541	$6,000	$55,131	$7,200	$112,635
$25	$3,000	$6,575	$4,500	$15,409	$6,000	$33,177	$7,500	$68,914	$9,000	$140,794
$50	$6,000	$13,151	$9,000	$30,818	$12,000	$66,354	$15,000	$137,828	$18,000	$281,589
$75	$9,000	$19,726	$13,500	$46,227	$18,000	$99,531	$22,500	$206,742	$27,000	$422,383
$100	$12,000	$26,302	$18,000	$61,637	$24,000	$132,707	$30,000	$275,656	$36,000	$563,177
$200	$24,000	$52,604	$36,000	$123,273	$48,000	$265,415	$60,000	$551,312	$72,000	$1,126,354
$300	$36,000	$78,905	$54,000	$184,910	$72,000	$398,122	$90,000	$826,968	$108,000	$1,689,531
$400	$48,000	$105,207	$72,000	$246,546	$96,000	$530,829	$120,000	$1,102,624	$144,000	$2,252,708
$500	$60,000	$131,509	$90,000	$308,183	$120,000	$663,537	$150,000	$1,378,280	$180,000	$2,815,885
$1,000	$120,000	$263,018	$180,000	$616,366	$240,000	$1,327,073	$300,000	$2,756,561	$360,000	$5,631,770
$2,000	$240,000	$526,036	$360,000	$1,232,731	$480,000	$2,654,147	$600,000	$5,513,122	$720,000	$11,263,541
$3,000	$360,000	$789,055	$540,000	$1,849,097	$720,000	$3,981,220	$900,000	$8,269,682	$1,080,000	$16,895,311

Invest Each Month	Total $ Invested	Principal & Interest 35 yrs	Total $ Invested	Principal & Interest 40 yrs	Total $ Invested	Principal & Interest 45 yrs	Total $ Invested	Principal & Interest 50 yrs
$10	$4,200	$114,148	$4,800	$230,467	$5,400	$464,424	$6,000	$934,997
$15	$6,300	$171,223	$7,200	$345,700	$8,100	$696,636	$9,000	$1,402,495
$20	$8,400	$228,297	$9,600	$460,933	$10,800	$928,849	$12,000	$1,869,993
$25	$10,500	$285,371	$12,000	$576,167	$13,500	$1,161,061	$15,000	$2,337,491
$50	$21,000	$570,742	$24,000	$1,152,334	$27,000	$2,322,121	$30,000	$4,674,983
$75	$31,500	$856,113	$36,000	$1,728,500	$40,500	$3,483,182	$45,000	$7,012,474
$100	$42,000	$1,141,484	$48,000	$2,304,667	$54,000	$4,644,243	$60,000	$9,349,965
$200	$84,000	$2,282,969	$96,000	$4,609,334	$103,000	$9,288,486	$120,000	$18,699,931
$300	$126,000	$3,424,453	$144,000	$6,914,001	$162,000	$13,932,729	$180,000	$28,049,896
$400	$168,000	$4,565,938	$192,000	$9,218,668	$213,000	$18,576,971	$240,000	$37,399,862
$500	$210,000	$5,707,422	$240,000	$11,523,335	$273,000	$23,221,214	$300,000	$46,749,827
$1,000	$420,000	$11,414,844	$480,000	$23,046,671	$540,000	$46,422,428	$600,000	$93,499,654
$2,000	$840,000	$22,829,688	$960,000	$46,093,341	$1,080,000	$92,884,857	$1,200,000	$186,999,309
$3,000	$1,260,000	$34,244,532	$1,440,000	$69,140,012	$1,620,000	$139,327,285	$1,800,000	$280,498,963

The purpose of all examples in this book is to encourage you to begin investing.
The calculations are from an interactive online calculator and are not intended to provide investment advice.

Time really is magic. The cost of waiting **only** two years to begin investing is shown here. Are you investing yet?

Invested @ 15% compounded annually

$ INVESTED	START NOW 30 YR RETURN	POSTPONE 2 YEARS 28 YR RETURN	COST OF WAITING
$50/mo	$281,587	$211,867	$69,720
$100/mo	$563,179	$423,738	$139,441
$200/mo	$1,126,352	$847,472	$278,880
$500/mo	$2,815,885	$2,118,684	$697,201

Resources
Books
> *The Richest Man in Babylon* by George S. Clason

> *Turning Passions into Profits, 3 Steps to Wealth and Power*
>   by Chris Howard

Breakthrough to Success Weekend
    chrishoward.com/bts/?af=211

Online calculators
    mindyourfinances.com/calculators/savings-calculator
    dinkytown.net/java/WaitCost.html

> *Financial freedom is not a matter of chance.*
> *It is a matter of choice. My choice.*

Chapter 3 | *How to Find the Money NOW to Start Saving and Investing*

Wealthy thoughts, beliefs, feelings, words, and actions will help create a life of abundance and opportunity for you. Your future, your destiny, is up to you—not anyone else. You can begin to create options for yourself, buy a car, take a trip to Europe, buy a house, finance any dream, or create financial freedom. You can start building your dreams now. Your future is in your hands. What can you do right now to find the money to invest?

You get to decide what kind of life you will have and how you can make the world a better place. You can begin right now!

> *What you need is time and consistency.*

Characteristics of Millionaires
$ They live below their income and invest the rest
$ They have goals and commit to them
$ They watch for bargains
$ They never pay interest by buying on time
$ They eliminate unnecessary expenses (needs versus wants)
$ They create their own wealth; 99% are self-made
$ They do not show off their wealth
$ They do not pay unnecessary taxes
$ They pay their children salaries, not allowances
$ They do not tell their children that they are wealthy
$ Their teach their children to be financially self-sufficient at an early age
$ They manage their time, energy, and money carefully

Begin Your Journey to Financial Freedom

Have a family meeting and agree that you want to be one of the four people out of 100 who live and retire rich. You must agree to spend less than you take in. Agree that you can never reach your goals while using credit or being in constant debt. Credit and debt are like drugs; they give you short-term gain and long-term pain.

$ Spend less than you earn.

$ Question every purchase. Ask yourself, "Is this a need or a want?" If it's a want, don't waste your money.

$ Make a list of the ways, as a family, you can reduce spending. See *2000 Ways to Lower Living Expenses* in the Appendix for ideas.

$ Stop giving the IRS interest-free loans for 15 months: 80% of Americans overpay their income taxes by $2,500 or more each year.

> If you are among them, go to your Human Resources Department tomorrow. Change your W-4 form to increase your dependents to whatever number is needed so your annual refund is about $100 to avoid penalty for underpayment. This will give you $200 each month to invest and/or apply to any debt. If invested at 15% compounded semimonthly for 30 years, you'd have $1,404,244. That's an additional $46,808 for each of those 30 years, or an income stream of $3,900 a month.

$ Choose to become debt-free. See Chapter 8 for details.

$ Simplify your life by having only one credit card; destroy the other 13.2 cards.

By now you have a stack of money by following the above advice. Here's what you do with your newfound money. Divide the money in two. The first half goes to start your 401(k) plan at work. About 80% of employers now have a 401(k) or a 503(b) programs, and 50% of those have matching money, which makes your annual return 100%. This happens year after year. The other half you pay on any remaining credit card debt. Currently you pay 145% interest per year on your credit cards (more later on both your 401(k) and credit cards).

Purchase your home. Owning your home, paid for or not, will make you a multimillionaire using an interest-only mortgage. See Chapter 9.

When you rent, you make other people millionaires.

> $1,000 rent per month from age 23-88
> = 65 years
> x $12,000 per year
> = $780,000

The only thing you have to show for your $780,000 is 780 worthless rent receipts.

$ Increase the family's income to invest more in your 401(k) and toward paying off your credit card debt. This can be achieved by starting a home-based business, having the children get jobs, increasing the parents' salary and/or hours.

Now, and every succeeding month, more and more money will become free from the sources listed above. Split the increased savings between your 401(k) payroll contribution until it is fully funded and your credit card debt until it is completely paid off. In Chapter 12, many other investments will be presented.

Three Most Important Investments of Your Life

$ **Purchase your home** as quickly as possible using interest-only mortgage.

$ **Omit credit card debt** because you are paying 145% interest on everything you purchase with a credit card if your balance isn't paid in full monthly.

$ **Start your 401(k)** as soon as possible because this gives you a 100% annual interest return year after year.

Remember: *Things* don't always bring happiness. In fact, the more things you have, the more boring life becomes. Please read the fascinating article "The Quest For The Simple Life" in *Money*, August 2006, page 135, and see the radical improvement it made for a family of six.

Features of All Successful Saving and Investment Plans

$ **Pay Yourself First**
You are the most important component. Without you, no one else would get paid. Consequently, respect yourself. Pay yourself first. Even if you begin with only 1%, then move to 15% as quickly as you can.

$ **Become Debt-Free Fast**
Chapter 8 gives detailed help.

$ **Pay Cash**
Operate on a 100% cash basis. Do not accrue more debt.

$ **Have More Money to Save and Invest for Yourself**
Refer to the Appendix for *2000 Ways to Lower Living Expenses* and *2000 Ways to Lower Income Taxes*.

$ **Expect a Good Yield**
Throughout this book you are going to get substantial help on this gigantic, important subject.

$ **Time Is the Key**
You cannot wait until six months prior to retirement and expect miracles. Start early in life. Chapter 2 covered this critical subject.

$ **Invest, Invest, Invest**
Chapter 12 is devoted to investing. Remember that 98.6% of all wealthy people have two types of investments in their portfolio—securities (stocks and other paper money) and real estate. See on the next page how stock ownership has increased since 1980.

$ **Compound Your Investments**
Compounding is the eighth wonder of the world! Review Chapter 2.

$ **Diversify Your Investments**
First focus on the urgent priority of getting out of debt. Afterward, diversification becomes exceedingly important.

$ **Focus on Wealth Creation and Preservation**

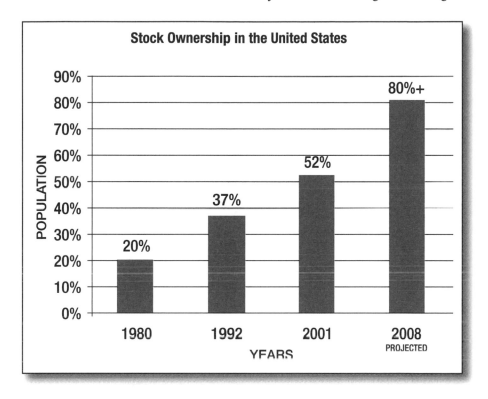

Stocks Paying Dividends Now in Vogue

Since the capital gains tax on dividend income was reduced to 15%, a gigantic drop, corporate America took a hard look at increasing dividends. As a result, companies started to pay and/or increase dividends to their shareholders on a monthly, quarterly, semiannual, or annual basis.

Generally speaking, dividend-paying stocks have a higher total yield. Monthly dividends are paid by real estate investment trusts RIETs, by many Canadian trusts, and by many of the 168 investment categories. The next three pages list several dozen of the thousands of companies paying dividends. To find more, look in the business section of your newspaper and on the Internet for companies paying 10%-30% dividends.

LOAN or OWN

All investments are divided into two major categories—loan or own. You loan money when you invest in bank passbook accounts, regular bank savings accounts, treasury bills, tax-free bonds, CDs, etc. These investors take

High-Dividend Stocks

STOCK (ON NYSE UNLESS NOTED)	DIVIDEND YIELD
Temp Emerging	29.6%
Frontline LTD (FRO)	19.8%
Harvest Energy	17.2%
Dominion Warrior Trust	15.9%
Canetic Resources	15.3%
Pengrowth Energy	14.9%
ING Clarion Global (IGR)	14.6%
Advantage Energy	14.0%
Nicholas-Applegate International & Pennstrategy Fund	14.0%
BP Prudhoe	13.9%
Rio Vista Energy Partners (RVEP)	13.6%
Annual Mortgage Management Inc	13.6%
Alpine Dyn (ADVX)	13.5%
Prime West Energy	13.3%
Anworth Mortgage Asset Corp.	12.9%
Eagle (Hasdag)	13.0%
Capstone Mortgage	13.0%
National Health Investors	12.6%
Boulder Growth and Income	11.9%
Nucor Elks (EKN)	11.5%
Penn West Energy	11.4%
MAG First Trust	11.3%
Telecomunicacoes de Sao Paulo [Brazilian Telephone]	11.2%
Salomon Brothers Emerging Markets	11.0%
ARC Energy	11.0%
Telecom of New Zealand	10.8%
Provident Energy Trust	10.7%
Mesalic Trust	10.4%
Thornburg Mortgage	10.3%
Big Rock Brewery	10.2%
Hormel Foods	10.0%

High-Dividend Stocks

STOCK (ON **NYSE** UNLESS NOTED)	DIVIDEND YIELD
Atlantic Power	9.9%
Calpine Power	9.9%
Enerplus Resources	9.8%
Ferrell Gas	9.3%
Arc Energy	9.2%
Arctic Glacier	8.7%
Great Northern Iron Ore	8.7%
Boralex Power	8.5%
FairPoint Communications	8.1%
Centerplate	8.0%
Plum Creek Timber	8.0%
Armadillo Timber Stock #7	8.0%
Coinmach Service Corp (Amer:DRY)	7.9%
Iowa Telecom	7.9%
B&G Foods (Amex:BGF)	7.8%
Duke Energy	7.8%
ING Prime Rate Trust	7.7%
Enbridge Partners	7.7%
Hartford Capital	7.6%
Alliance Resource Partners L.P.	7.4%
Otelco (Amer:OTT)	7.0%
Wells Real Estate Investment Trust (REIT)	7.0%
Sturm Rugers	7.0%
Dow Jones 30 Industrial Averages	2.0%-6.8%
Virginia Electric and Power	6.5%
Alliance Capital	6.0%
Eastman Kodak	5.9%
Consolidated Edison (NY Utilities)	5.9%
SBC Communications	5.1%
Glaxo Smith Kline	5.1%
Dow Chemicals	5.0%

High Dividend Stocks

STOCK (ON NYSE UNLESS NOTED)	DIVIDEND YIELD
Southern Utilities	4.8%
California Water Service Group	3.9%
Schering-Plough	3.7%
Genuine Parts	3.5%
York Water	3.4%
Quaker Chemicals	3.3%
DuPont Chemicals	3.3%
General Electric	3.0%
Merck Drug	2.7%

Dividend rates listed are no guarantee of future performance. Factual material has been obtained from sources believed to be reliable, and is not guaranteed. All examples are for illustrative purposes only and are not to be construed as recommendations, advice, or tax counsel. The author and publisher are not engaged in rendering legal, accounting, or other professional service. If legal or other expert assistance is required, the author and publisher strongly recommend that the reader should contact his or her own professional advisors.

"If a business does well, the stock eventually follows."
WARREN BUFFETT

the money you loan them, reinvest it, and make a nice profit for themselves.

When you own your investments, you take possession of the investments themselves, such as real estate, stock shares, precious metals, commodities, etc. In most cases, your returns are far greater when you own your investments than when you just loan out your money.

My goal is for you to have the most money possible in the shortest time possible.

> *"Most people think they want more money than they do and settle for a lot less than they could have."*
> EARL NIGHTINGALE

Financial Freedom Planning While You Are Still Young

What if you were to wake up every morning and had the choice to be able to do whatever you wanted? What would that take? To be age 65?

No!

It's not age, it's money. Yes, the green stuff. The money to do what you want, when you want, and with whom you want. Imagine if you could create the funds so that you could live the life of your dreams sooner rather than later? Choose financial freedom!

If you are still young, retirement may seem like a long way away. And if you work hard for your money, instead of having your money work hard for you, it will be a long way away. And, I would love to see you retire 20 years from your wedding date with a net worth of $10 million. If this is your dream, then it is imperative to list your goals and plan for retirement 90 days before your engagement to make certain that you have financial intimacy.

As I stated in the introduction, you are on your own for your retirement planning. Fortunately, time is on your side and a great ally if you are still young. The habit of saving and investing for your financial freedom is much easier to develop when you are young and if you follow your goals earnestly.

Do not be like Jackie Mason, who said, "I have enough money to last me the rest of my life, unless I buy something."

In closing this chapter, I want to extend to you a wish for a great deal of success as you plan for your fabulous financial future, and I leave you with these words of wisdom.

Success

The dictionary is the only place where "success" comes before "work." You need to wake up, get up, and get going. The foundation for a better tomorrow must be laid today.

The ladder of success must be set upon something solid before you can start to climb. It cannot be climbed with your hands in your pockets. To get through any journey, take only one step at a time, and keep on stepping.

Resources
Book
> *Preferreds: Wall Street's Best-Kept Secret* by Kenneth G. Winans
>> PreferredsTheBook.com

For the serious investor
> *Morningstar Dividend Investor,* a monthly newsletter
> 866-608-9570

Online calculator
> fandktitle.com/calcs/allcalcs/invest_return_calculator.htm

Web site
> kiplinger.com/links/w4

> *"Reading will give you knowledge,*
> *action will give you experience,*
> *results will give you confidence."*
> LORAL LANGEMEIER

Chapter 4 | *Your Best Financial Decision— Selecting the Right Mate!*

Happiness

We convince ourselves that life will be better after we get married, have a baby, and then another. Then we are frustrated that the kids aren't old enough, and we'll be more content when they are. After that, we're frustrated that we have teenagers to deal with. We will certainly be happy when they are out of that stage. We tell ourselves that our life will be complete when our spouse gets his or her act together, when we get a nicer car, are able to go on a nice vacation, or when we retire.

The truth is, there's no better time to be happy than right now. If not now, when? Your life will always be filled with challenges. It's best to admit this to yourself and decide to be happy anyway.

One of my favorite quotes comes from Alfred D. Souza: "For a long time it had seemed to me that life was about to begin–real life. But there was always some obstacle in the way, something to be gotten through first, some unfinished business, time still to be served, or debt to be paid. Then life would begin. At last it dawned on me that these obstacles were my 'life'. This perspective has helped me to see that there is no way to happiness. Happiness is the way."

So, treasure every moment. And if you share it with someone special, treasure it even more.

Eighty percent of success in marriage depends on whom you marry. I am going to talk about divorce first, then marriage. Why marriage and divorce in a book on finances? Simple. The average divorce causes the greatest financial crisis in most families and it lasts a lifetime, with no or very little chance of anyone involved becoming a millionaire.

> *Marry the one you cannot live without,*
> *not the one you think you can live with.*

Major Reasons for Divorce

Depending on what book you read, or what research you review, you will find one thing in common. Money problems cause 75%-85% of all divorces. Here are additional reasons.

- Stress
- Finances, which cause stress
- Children – some naive parents think having children will solve their problems; in reality, the problems are compounded with more stress and financial issues
- Unexpressed anger, which leads to resentment
- Majoring on the minors and minoring on the majors
- No longer investing time with each other
- Lack of respect, trust, and love
- Lack of true communication at the heart level

Results of Divorce

Dan Rather made a statement about the horrors of divorce based on actual studies and facts: "20,000,000 children with no fathers results in #1 cause of crime, #1 cause of poverty, #1 cause of loneliness and depression."

- The biggest killer of marriages is lack of money.
- The U.S. leads the world in divorce.
- Only 14% of children in the U.S. spend the first three years in full-time care of their parents.
- Only 51% of all children live in a home with two parents.
- Children from divorced parents are affected for life.
- Divorce inflicts terrible pain on its victims.
    - ~ Husband and wife suffer dramatically
    - ~ 90% of children suffer acute shock
    - ~ 50% of children feel rejected and abandoned
    - ~ 50% of fathers never see their children after 3 years
    - ~ 37% of children were more unhappy after 5 years
    - ~ Most children are affected for life

- These hurting children are all around us.
- Millions of single mothers are left to struggle to care for the children, to work one or more jobs for an average of 18 hours per day, six days per week. All this just to survive.
- Many single parents end up on several types of welfare while the rest pay higher taxes.

How to Have a Great Marriage—If You Plan to Be Married

Remember, 80% of your success in marriage depends on whom you marry.

Four Ways to Stay Happily Married

- 90 days before your engagement is the most important time of your life. That is the time to get serious, talk, and ask questions of your soon-to-be spouse.
  - ~ Review each other's goals in life.
  - ~ Review each other's finances.
  - ~ Talk about love-intimacy compatibility.
  - ~ Talk about financial-intimacy compatibility.

  If you are compatible—great. If not, walk away—fast.

- Order 2 free questionnaires from *Adventist Contact* (see resources). Fill out separately, then swap. Share and discuss with each other. If any deal breakers show up, then part as friends.

- Take a marriage compatibility test from a local college or university. If you find you are not compatible, give each other a big hug and kiss, and go your separate ways.

➡ **If you are compatible, congratulations!**
  Now ask the question and become engaged!

- Arrange for a three-month premarital class from a pastor or rabbi, either at your church or synagogue, or one nearby.

- Both boyfriend and girlfriend have a marketable trade, skill, or profession prior to marriage.

- Wife works away from home first six years, longer if desired.
- Live off one salary and invest 100% of the second.

    It's easy to live off one salary when you have reduced taxes, no children, no debt, no instant gratification, and no interest payments.

- Plan to retire 20 years from your wedding date as a multimillionaire worth $10 million. See Chapter 5.
- Very important to wait six years prior to having children

    ~ Most divorces happen in first 3.5 years

    ~ Need time to adjust to each other

    ~ Need time to enjoy each other

    ~ Need time to get your life organized

    ~ Need time to get finances and investments in order

    Remember—if you have children, your life will change drastically forever. Do you have time for children?

    A mother was so busy that when she asked her child what he wanted for Christmas, the child requested six one-hour gift certificates of mother's time.

By following these suggestions, you will drastically improve your chances of staying married. And you can have a great, joyful, and happy marriage.

Married or Not…

$ Pay yourself first. Remember, "A portion of all I earn is mine to keep." Use your investment money only for investing.

$ Save, Save, Save. Be different from the average American.

$ Invest, Invest, Invest.

$ Safeguard your name and credit until you are a millionaire. Then you won't need any more credit.

$ Expect high yields, an average of 15% compounded annually on all your investments for life. See Chapter 12.

$ Legally reduce your income taxes. This equals wealth for you. Almost 82% of all taxpayers overpay taxes every year.

$ Pay cash for everything except your home and investments. Paying interest lowers your standard of living.

Create Partnership

When preparing to write this book, for months I gathered and filed all the information about the various topics. When it came time to put my thoughts on paper, I sat down, picked up a folder, focused on what I wanted to say, and wrote the chapter. My wife would come into the office and it could be five minutes until I realized she was standing there. I was focused. I wanted to have the chapter finished, and nothing was going to deter me from achieving that result. Even if it took several days, 10-12 hours a day, my focus was on finishing that chapter.

Then I passed the chapters on to my associate for her input. And I thought she'd handle the chapters the same way—begin with chapter 1 and work on it until it was finished, move to chapter 2, and then to chapter 3, etc. When that didn't happen, I was frustrated.

Fortunately, she explained to me, kindly, that she works differently. She'd work on a chapter for a while, then another, and then another. In between, she'd do her laundry, fix a meal, go for a walk. This, I said seemed, illogical.

She then shared that there are instinctual differences between men and women, which—when understood—allows for better communication and the ability to create partnerships, in romance, families, and work environment. Different is not good or bad, it is not right or wrong, it's just different.

And one of those differences is how we focus. She explained that I was single-focused—focused on a result (finishing the chapter), and using my track vision (what was needed to complete the chapter). She, on the other hand, has diffuse awareness, which means to pour out in every direction. This is what allows her to focus on more than one thing at a time.

Now this was interesting and I asked for another example. Knowing I like to drive, she said, "You're on a single-lane road focused on what's in front of you, and I'm on a ten-lane freeway able to switch lanes while still heading the same direction." Now this made sense!

Then she said, "I've also learned not to interrupt a man when he is focused. And a win is that when he's focused on me, I know he's 100% present!"

I asked her how she got to be so smart. She said that she'd taken a weekend class called *Celebrating Men Satisfying Women*® (see resources).

Recently, on *Oprah*, a lady shared how her marriage had not been good and they had not been intimate for more than a year. A week earlier, she had learned about the Universal Law of Attraction and realized she had focused on what was missing, what made her unhappy. She changed her focus to the good things—the great things—in her mate and her marriage. She began to express gratitude for everything in her life she liked and loved. There was almost an instant shift in their relationship. Her husband, with a big smile on his face, agreed. Just think, they were able to turn their marriage around in only a few days!

Isn't it amazing that in the two most important areas of our lives—finances and relationships—most of us have not had even one hour of training. This is crazy! This book will help with the finances. And there are lots of books, seminars, and workshops on how to create a great relationship, to listen with understanding (not just hearing), and to communicate so that each partner is heard. Invest in yourself and those you love.

Why Wait to Have Children

As I look back, it is 100% clear that the most enjoyable years of my married life were the first 10 years, from our honeymoon until our first child was born. Please understand, children are great and we were blessed to have a son and a daughter whom we love and enjoy. And it was never the same as when it was just the two of us.

My wife stayed at home after working 12 years. Looking back, I would give anything if she would have discontinued her teaching career when she became pregnant with our first child. This is why I have encouraged thousands of couples to wait six years after the wedding to have their first child. That way they could invest one entire salary for those six years and then she could stay home to raise the children—and with a full salary for life. See Chapter 5.

With this plan, the wife does not work away from the home, commute two to three hours per day, then come back home to hours more of work: shopping, cooking, laundry, cleaning, taking care of the children, all to the point of exhaustion.

When the wife is exhausted, how can anyone expect her to be the loving, intimate, sexy lady she really is? I read this in *Annie's Mailbox* in my local paper. "My wife and I have been married 20 years. The first 10 we did not have children, and during that time the sex was both great and plentiful. Since having kids there is a brief time once every couple of weeks. The rest of the time my wife is too tired or there are many other necessary things to be done."

Should You Have Children?

Are you positive you have the time, effort, love, and money to raise and train your children? The most difficult job in America is rearing children. Today 75% of children in the U.S. are left to grow up in front of the television, by their peers, or on the streets!

- 27% are from broken homes.
- 51% are from two-parent homes.
- The most difficult job in America is parenting.
- One in four U.S. children face hunger. Only twice in my life have I heard, "Have children only if you can afford them."
- "Parents have no right to bring children in the world to be a burden to others," wrote E. G. White. It is totally inconsiderate to have more children than you can afford. Do not expect the government, your neighbors, or your relatives to pay part or all of the cost of raising your children.
- Every couple should consider the cost of raising a child from conception to 18 years of age. According to recent statistics, the average cost is $485,000 to raise a boy and $520,000 for a girl.

    An 11-year-old boy asked his dad, "How much does it cost to get married?" The dad replied," I don't know, I am still paying."
- If you have children, teach them independence.

    Harvard University researchers found that the willingness and capacity to work in childhood is the most single important forerunner of good mental health in adulthood along with becoming a productive concerned citizen. Work in childhood was more important than social class, family situation, or even native intelligence.
- The greatest gift you can give your children is a solid education in financial management and good work ethics. It helps them and you. It is almost impossible to have wealth with dependent children.

- Enroll your children in money classes or financial camps for children. Give them instruction in money matters and they will be in the top 20% of all Americans.
- Teach the difference between cost and benefits, of wants versus needs, and how to make choices.

    Little 4-year-old Tommy was given a stick of candy by one of the clerks in the store. "What do you say now, Tommy?" his mother prompted. "Charge it," said Tommy.

Do not let anyone bug you about having children. Not all married couples decide to have children (that decision is yours only).

Keep the Sparkle, Romance, and Intimacy in Your Life

Recent research shows that healthy marriages contribute to good health, higher income, and more savings and investments. Social people tend to eat healthier, exercise more regularly, and live longer, happier lives.

- Treasure each day with your very special beloved.
- Take charge of your life.
- Plan your day to include time to enjoy one of the best-priced gifts in history—love-intimacy.
- Relax, be peaceful, and have a joyous life.
- Go on a four-day mini-honeymoon four times a year.

    That's right! Alternate who plans the location so that it will be a surprise to your spouse. Many resorts and nice hotels have special rates on weekends. You can have an outstanding time without breaking the bank. If you have children, leave them with the grandparents or good friends.

- For the wife, increase the surprise by purchasing new lingerie at least every other time. WOW, that will give your hubby something else to look forward to!
- Choose relaxation, peace, and well-being.
- Create the time and space where both partners can cuddle their spouse's nude, warm, delightful body before falling off to sleep for a great night's rest. WOW, it gives me goosebumps just thinking about it.

- Take time to give your spouse a massage.

  According to the medical experts, massages have at least a dozen medical benefits, including the most important aspect of the warmth of your hands on a warm, appreciating body. You get the point.
- Have a job you love.
- Work from home if you can. If not, find a job of your choice close to home. Spend the commute time with your family.
- Leave your work at work.
- Work smarter, not harder.
- Simplify your life wherever possible.
- Eliminate the average of 14.2 credit cards to one and pay it in full monthly.
- Automate everything possible to save time and stress. One example is bill paying. Pay on your computer, credit card, or check-o-matic directly paid by your bank checking account.
- Focus on having enough rest. Exhaustion equals stress. Stress brings on anger and anger causes distance in your marriage.
- Be kind, considerate, and gentle with each other.
- Remember your spouse's birthday and your anniversary.
- Husbands, surprise your sweet wife with flowers.
- Keep your life simple, uncluttered, and stress-free.
- Shut off the telephones at 6 p.m.

  Tell family and close friends that the evenings are your private, family time. Finally, many couples are doing this.
- Train the children to get to bed early and stay in bed.
- Good health affects your entire life, including your sex life.
- All the money in the world will not bring back ruined health.
- Drink five to eight glasses of water daily.

  It will help maintain your ideal body weight, improve kidney function, and keep your body hydrated. A large-scale study over the past six years says that drinking five to eight glasses of water per day reduces fatal heart attacks in men by 54% and women 41%. Other liquids

such as juice, milk, coffee, and alcohol had the opposite effect, almost doubling the risk of heart attacks.
- Live a healthy lifestyle, which includes exercise, eight hours of sleep, and proper nutrition to maintain ideal weight.
  The greatest health book I have seen is *Health Power: Health by Choice, Not Chance*. (See Resources) It's an easy, quick read, can change your life, and help you stay healthy.

Happily married couples take time for each other, relax together, show each other respect, and have physical affection for each other.

Remember, you need love intimacy and financial intimacy. If you have children, you need to add family intimacy—love, closeness, and being as one.

Resources
Books
Health Power: Health by Choice, Not Chance
   by Dr. Arleen Lundington and Dr. Hans Diehl
   909-796-7676
   chipheart.com (click on resources)

The Five Love Languages by Gary Chapman

Celebrating Men, Satisfying Women®
   understandmen.com/?SSAID=197150
   understandmen.com/cmsw/index.html?SSAID=197150

Questionnaire, Free
   Adventist Contact, PO Box 5419, Takoma Park, MD 20913
   301-589-4440

The reason the other side of the fence appears to be greener is because you have not watered your side of the fence.

| Chapter 5 | *Be Worth $10 Million—*
20 Years From
Your Wedding Day |

These are the easiest ways to become a multimillionaire! Before you become engaged, decide together to become financially free.

Reduce the Cost of Your Wedding

Forty-five billion dollars was spent on weddings in 2004. In the United States, the average cost of a wedding on the east and west coasts is $38,000; the national average is $26,000. The bridal gown and reception generally are the most expensive items.

After receiving my masters, my first job was the director of a college food service. During those four years, my associates and I became well-known for the gorgeous wedding receptions we would create. From all my experience, you can have an eloquent wedding for thousands less than the national average.

If you and your fiancée have the goal to be financially free, spend less and still have an awesome wedding. Be creative! Purchase the book *A Simply Beautiful Wedding* by Eileen Silva Kindig. It shows how to have a magnificent wedding for much less so that you will have a sizeable nest egg to start or continue with your investment program. If you save $15,000 on your wedding and invest it, in just 30 years you would have almost $1 million!

Invest one time @ 15% compounded annually

YRS	$15,000	$20,000
10	$60,683	$80,911
20	$245,498	$327,330
30	$993,176	$1,324,235
40	$4,017,953	$5,357,270

Reduce Your Taxes Legally

Another major way to become a millionaire is to reduce your income tax and invest the tax savings yourself. The average household spends $18,750 in taxes per year. Reduce them in half and invest the $9,375. Chapter 16 is devoted to this topic in detail. In addition, the Appendix has *2000 Ways to Lower Income Taxes*.

Annual Taxes per family	$18,750
50% taxes saved per year and invested	$9,375

$9,375 invested yearly @ 15% compounded annually

	TOTAL INVESTED	PRINCIPAL/INTEREST
20 years	$187,500	$1,104,470
30 years	$281,150	$4,687,096
40 years	$375,000	$19,180,817

First invest in your 401(k) and other pension plans. Then start a home business, even if it's part-time, as it will allow you to take advantage of many tax savings.

For 25 years, I owned several farms in Vermont while I lived and worked in California. Those farms gave me excellent income-tax deductions, making it possible to legally reduce my income taxes. Instead of paying unnecessary income tax, I invested that money. Yes, and I still paid my fair share of taxes. Did you know there are 72 different taxes in a loaf of bread?

Eliminate Paying Interest

When you pay interest on loans and credit cards others become millionaires instead of yourself. The only interest you should ever pay for is for investments—period! It is tax deductible and will save you money, so you will have more to invest. For everything else, pay cash. See how simple it is to become debt-free in Chapter 8.

Before my dear, beautiful girlfriend and I were married, we agreed to pay interest only on money for investments. Now decades later, no interest was ever paid. You can choose to do the same whether married or not.

The average household spends (actually wastes) $10,875 interest per year on 14.2 credit cards and loans. Keep this money and invest it for yourself.

$10,875 invested yearly @ 15% compounded annually

	TOTAL INVESTED	PRINCIPAL/INTEREST
20 years	$217,500	$1,281,185
30 years	$326,250	$5,437,031
40 years	$435,000	$22,249,748

Invest Second Salary

For numerous logical reasons listed in Chapter 3, I strongly recommend waiting six years before having children. By doing so, both husband and wife can work full-time. Choose to live on one salary and invest the entire other salary. In six years you will have $261,737 and a couple of choices.

You could choose to have a perpetual income of $39,261 created from the interest and dividends so you can stay home and raise your own children. What a blessing that would be for your family—and the nation!

Another choice would be to keep the interest invested and compounding and in 14 short years (20 years total), your investment from six year's salary would be worth $1.8 million. Now that's exciting!

$26,000 invested yearly for 6 years @ 15% compounded annually

	TOTAL INVESTED	PRINCIPAL/INTEREST
20 years	$156,000	$1,851,974
30 years	$156,000	$7,492,268
40 years	$156,000	$30,310,402

401(k) Investment Program

The value of a 401(k) investment program is so awesome, that when you and your spouse graduate from college, I urge you to consider the following:

$ Select the best job which has the best 401(k) plan and contribute 100% to your plan. Remember, 80% of all companies offer a 401(k) plan and 50% of those will contribute to your plan—free money for you.

$ Live as close to your job as possible in order to reduce your commute time, automobile expenses, and the wear and tear on yourself. Choose to be rested and to spend lots of quality time together, rather than in commuter traffic.

Let me blow your mind! You can have $1,889,888 in 20 years with a yearly cost of only $5,700. "How's that possible?"

First, assume you fully contribute to a 401(k) for 20 years. Remember, you are not out-of-pocket the full $15,000. Your employer contributes $5,000 per year. And, if you are in the 43% federal and state income tax bracket, the government reduces your taxes by $4,300 a year. So, instead of $15,000, you are only out of pocket $5,700 per year.

	Yearly Contribution
Paid into your 401(k) investment program	$15,000
Less employers contribution	-$5,000
	$10,000
Less income tax deduction	-$4,300
Actual out of payroll cost	$ 5,700

Just think, as a payroll deduction each paycheck, in 20 years you will have invested out-of-pocket only $114,000 ($5,700 per year) while the investment increased to $1,889,888 ($15,000 invested per year).

$625 invested semimonthly @ 15% compounded semimonthly

	TOTAL INVESTED	PRINCIPAL/INTEREST
20 years	$300,000	$1,889,888
30 years	$450,000	$8,776,530
40 years	$600,000	$39,496,576

Free Money–Invest Semimonthly versus Annually

Another gigantic aspect of the miracle of compound interest is the free money you can make if you invest semimonthly or monthly instead of yearly.

Payroll deduction ($625 SEMIMONTHLY)/20 yrs	$1,889,888
Invest $15,000 once per year/20 yrs	$1,767,152
Added investment income	$122,736

This is the power of money making money! Compounding is earning interest on the principal **and** the accumulating interest.

Look at what consistent investing means to your financial freedom. Take $122,736 and divide by 20 (number of years). This give you $6,136 extra, free money per year invested!

And if you are married, each of you can contribute $15,000 per year to a 401(k) so you can double the investment returns shown.

Additional Money to Invest

$ **Reduce income tax refund**
   Add $2,400 back into your paycheck and invest each pay period.

$ **Interest-only mortgage**
   ~ $8,000 yearly tax savings on $300,000 home loan
      with 6% interest and 44.3% tax bracket
   ~ $500 average lower monthly payment

$ **Eliminate recommended cash cushion**
   Have a home equity loan established for emergencies.

Summary of Investment Returns

So 20 years from your wedding, you are a multimillionaire! This is the miracle of compound interest. You can now choose to "retire" wealthy while young.

	20 YEARS	30 YEARS	40 YEARS
WEDDING SAVINGS	$245,498	$993,176	$4,017,953
REDUCE INCOME TAX	$1,104,470	$4,687,096	$19,180,817
ELIMINATE INTEREST	$1,281,185	$5,437,031	$22,249,748
SALARY #2	$1,851,974	$7,492,268	$30,310,402
401(K)	$1,889,888	$8,776,530	$39,496,576
INCOME TAX REFUND	$302,382	$1,404,244	$6,319,452
INTEREST-ONLY MORTGAGE			
TAX SAVINGS	$942,481	$3,999,655	$16,367,631
LOWER PAYMENT	$757,977	$3,504,910	$15,701,878
$25,000 CUSHION	$409,163	$1,655,294	$6,696,588
TOTAL	$8,785,018	$37,950,204	$160,341,045

Remember, I said you would be worth $10 million 20 years from your wedding date. The other $1.23 million will come from the significant financial solutions and options given in the rest of the book. Choose two or three from Chapter 11 that are best for you and your family. And consider investing in a second 401(k).

Results When You Bless Your Children

After careful consideration, you and your spouse decide to have children and you want to give them the best life possible. You want them to have a great financial foundation.

What if you invested money for your children beginning at birth? What would the results be when they are 22? 45? Please consider this overview and see Chapter 10 for the details. Imagine what your child's life would be like with this awesome financial base! What a wonderful gift and legacy you would give, as you bless your children and even your grandchildren!

Amount Invested	Total $ Invested	Principal & Interest at age 22	Principal & Interest at age 45
$500 ONE TIME AT BIRTH, BABY SHOWER	$500	$10,822	$269,385
$600/yr (age 1-4) TOY MONEY-GRANDPARENTS	$2,400	$42,644	$1,061,208
$800/yr (age 1-5) 100% CHILD'S CASH GIFTS	$4,000	$66,752	$1,661,558
$1,000/yr (age 6-11) 75% CASH GIFTS, HIRE CHILD	$6,000	$46,836	$1,165,807
$4,000/yr (age 12-18) CHILD'S ROTH IRA	$28,000	$89,037	$2,216,252
$4,000/yr (age 15-18) CHILD'S EXTRA WAGES	$16,000	$40,175	$1,000,006
$3,000/yr (age 19-22) CASH GIFTS, EXTRA WAGES	$12,000	$17,227	$428,805
Investment Results	**$68,900**	**$313,493**	**$6,637,214**

Resources
Book
   A Simply Beautiful Wedding by Eileen Silva Kindig

Online calculators
   mindyourfinances.com/calculators/savings-calculator
   fandktitle.com/calcs/allcalcs/invest_return_calculator.htm

Yes, you can achieve financial-intimacy!

| Chapter 6 | *Significantly Increase Your Income Now!* |

Invest Twice a Month Versus Once a Year

How would you like to earn $6,811 extra this year and every year thereafter with no time involvement?

$100 invested semimonthly @ 15% compounded semimonthly

	TOTAL INVESTED	PRINCIPAL/INTEREST
20 years	$48,000	$302,382
30 years	$72,000	$1,404,244

$2,400 invested yearly @ 15% compounded annually

	TOTAL INVESTED	PRINCIPAL/INTEREST
20 years	$48,000	$282,744
30 years	$72,000	$1,199,897

Total increase for 30 years is $204,347. Would you believe this yearly increase of $6,811 in your income is *without any lifestyle change*? This can be done automatically through your payroll deductions directly to your investments.

Imagine the results if you were to invest more?

Use Your Income Taxes for You

Do not overpay income taxes as most people do. According to the IRS, the average amount withheld for income taxes by employers has increased. In 2006 it was more than $2,500. Why would you give the IRS an ongoing tax-free loan of $2,500 and do so year after year? Would you believe that by reducing your tax withholding $200 per month you can have almost $2.9 million in 35 years with no lifestyle changes?

$100 invested semimonthly @ 15% compounded semimonthly

	TOTAL INVESTED	PRINCIPAL/INTEREST
20 years	$48,000	$302,382
25 years	$60,000	$656,443
30 years	$72,000	$1,404,244
35 years	$84,000	$2,983,648

Go to your Human Resource Department tomorrow and fill out a new W-4 form. Increase the number of personal exemptions to whatever number it takes to reduce your annual overpayment to just $100. Can you imagine having an extra $302,382 in just 20 years to add to your retirement fund?

Reduce your income tax legally and invest those monies for yourself. Chapter 13 is devoted to this topic. Let's make just one assumption—that you and your spouse were able to reduce your income tax yearly by $5,000 ($416 per month).

$208 invested semimonthly @ 15% compounded semimonthly

	TOTAL INVESTED	PRINCIPAL/INTEREST
20 years	$99,840	$628,955
30 years	$149,760	$2,920,829

Money for You Now

$ Begin today to lower your expenses. Did you realize you can lower many expenses without affecting your lifestyle? See Appendix for *2000 Ways to Lower Living Expenses.*

$ Check for lost assets now and quarterly thereafter. It's very important to make a list of every asset you have, complete with names, telephone numbers, etc. so they will be remembered. See Chapter 19 for the details.

$ Never pay retail.

$ Stay out of debt.

$ According to the IRS and others, 96 out of every 100 people reach retirement unprepared due to instant gratification. **Remember, is it a need or a want**?

$ Pay interest only on money for investments and your home mortgage. Why make other people millionaires when you could become a multimillionaire yourself? The average family pays almost $11,000 per year in interest alone; that's $916 per month.

$916 invested monthly @ 15% compounded monthly

	TOTAL INVESTED	PRINCIPAL/INTEREST
20 years	**$219,840**	**$1,388,615**

$ Reduce food expenditures by eating out less and *watching* your grocery list. Did you realize you can purchase foods with greater nutitional value for at least 25% less money per month?

$ Reduce entertainment costs by one-half and still enjoy life to the fullest.

$ Reduce utility costs by 25%. Free energy audits are available from either the utility companies or the city.

$ Reduce your transportation costs by $4,000 per year. This is the difference between purchasing a new car and a creampuff used car—clean, one owner, and low mileage.

$333 invested monthly @ 15% compounded monthly

	TOTAL INVESTED	PRINCIPAL/INTEREST
20 years	**$79,920**	**$504,813**

Assume you will own a car all your life, say for 70 years. (Not the same car, of course!) Using the same formula, your $4,000 annual savings would grow just a bit! This is as real as this book you are reading. WOW! Is the new car worth it?

$333 invested monthly @ 15% compounded monthly

	TOTAL INVESTED	PRINCIPAL/INTEREST
70 years	**$279,720**	**$917,789,900**

$ Review all insurance policies and reduce costs 15%-50%. If a policy is more than three years old, there's a good chance of having twice the coverage for the same cost. Or keep the same coverage and lower your monthly payment substantially.

$ Eliminate all tuition. See Chapter 10.

$ Increase yields on your investments to average 15% per year. You may be in retirement up to 50 years. Consequently, you will want to invest all your life. See Chapter 12.

$ Remember, 98.6% of all wealthy people have two types of assets in their portfolio: real estate and securities. Learn from the wealthy!

$ Choose two or three of the 80 proven ways to become a millionaire. See Chapter 11.

$ Convert earned income (salary and wages) into passive income (securities and other paper investments) or portfolio income (real estate, etc.) as soon as possible to lower income taxes.

General Tax Consequences of Four Types of Income

	Work Hard for Your Money	Money Working Hard for You		
	Salary or Wages	Portfolio Income (Securities)	Passive Income (Real Estate)	Self-Employed Income*
Income Assumed	$1,000	$1,000	$1,000	$1,000
Taxable	100%	15%	-0-	-0-
Tax due based on 30% F & S tax bracket	$300	$150	-0-	-0-
Net left after taxes	$700	$850	$1,000	$1,000

✻ There are no taxes at this point because if you are self-employed working out of your home, you have more income tax deductions than any other skill, trade, or profession, including almost $100,000 in tax-deductible pension plans alone.

$ Have children only if you can afford them.

> While I am on this subject, if you have children, do not push them into excellence while you ruin their health, your health, and your bank account. Almost weekly, there is an article in a magazine, newspaper, or on TV about how parents push their children into every sport that man can devise, music lessons, special computer classes, workshops, etc., and the negative impact it has on the children.

> Remember what I said earlier about simplifying your life. If you have children, this is the first place to start. Save your time, effort, and money. The best thing you can do for your children is to teach them to work at an early age. The benefits are many. See Chapter 10.

$ Cash is king! Pay cash for everything except investments.

> Generally you pay 5%-20% less for most major items you purchase when you offer cash now. Dozens of times in my life this has worked for me—be it a creampuff car to a number of pieces of property. Also, remember that your home is an investment.

$ Use leverage by borrowing money to invest or use your home equity line-of-credit.

> Talking about home equity line of credit, I always have the bank give me the maximum amount. I have increased my line-of-credit many times since it started in 1978 with $25,000, the maximum allowed at that time. Now the bank calls me and asks if I want to increase my line-of-credit. Of course, I always say, "Yes." What do I do with the money? I invest it at a higher interest rate and keep the difference to support my lifestyle.

> CONSIDER THIS. For years, the interest was 4%-5% on my home equity line and was 100% tax-deductible.
> The inflation rate averaged 4%.
> Between the two, I didn't pay anything for a very sizeable loan.
> It was like free money!

The Three Most Important Ways to Increase Your Income

$ Take out an interest-only home mortgage, invest the tax savings and lower monthly payments, and become a multimillionaire. See Chapter 9.

$ Eliminate credit card interest and fee payments. This costs you 145%. See Chapter 7.

$ Contribute to your 401(k) or 403(b). It will provide you with **100% return year after year** (reduced income tax, employer matching funds, and interest earned):

~ When you contribute the amount your employer will match, you have an instant 100% return.

~ If you contribute 10% of a $70,000 salary, your employer matches 3% (free money to you), and the interest earned is 15%, your money will double in one year.

~ Start today. The longer you wait, the more money you leave on the table. The projected future value of a 10% contribution will **cost you $70,438 for every year you delay investing**.

Resources

Free evaluation of insurance policies
    Allen Kaye, 800-662-5433

401(k)
    why401k.com

Online calculators
    mindyourfinances.com/calculators/savings-calculator
    fandktitle.com/calcs/allcalcs/invest_return_calculator.htm

> *Do not follow where the path may lead.*
> *Go instead where there is no path and leave a trail.*

Chapter 7

Credit Card Debt Is Compounding Interest in Reverse

Compounding can work against you. When you borrow money, compounding works against you by taking more of your money, sometimes far more than the amount you initially borrowed.

How can credit cards cost you at least 145% interest annually? It's simple.

100%	Interest lost by not having money to fund your 401(k), which gives you 100% annual return year after year.
30%	Credit card interest charge If you are late one time, your rate increases. If late again, the rate increases again. When you carry a balance, interest is charged on already-accrued interest. (Many companies charge up to 40%.)
15%	Increased cost by not paying cash Studies show that the average shopper spends 15% more when credit cards are used instead of cash.
145%	**What credit card debt really costs**

Learn to Love Being Debt-Free

Sixty-eight percent of all households carry balances on their credit cards. I hope you are not one of them. Having credit card debt makes the credit card companies wealthy; meanwhile, it puts you in a financial hole.

Americans are kept in bondage and slavery. The average household uses 14.2 credit cards. Four billion more cards are being sent out this year. In 2005 there were an estimated 4 billion credit cards in Americans' wallets.

Radio, television, and telemarketing want you to spend more money and pay interest. Fight back by becoming debt-free and staying that way.

Poor habits are learned very young. One mother shared, "When I heard the sound of the ice cream wagon's bell and saw my front door wide open, I suspected that my 2 ½-year-old son had run outside. As I caught up with him, I saw he was clutching my credit card in his hand."

Using Credit Is Renting a False Lifestyle You Cannot Afford!

The main cause of financial failure is instant gratification, buying what you want when you want it, whether or not you have the money.

- Living in too large a home with a mortgage beyond your means
- Making payments on one or more expensive cars
- Using your credit cards to take expensive vacations
- Taking your good car in to have the oil changed and coming home with a new $25,000 automobile and five years of payments
- Buying $2,000 of furniture on credit
  If you pay the minimum due each month, it will take you 30 years to pay off the loan for a total of $10,000—five times the original amount (and there's a good chance that the furniture is no longer in use, either).

You get the point. Credit is like a drug—short-term gain with long-term pain.

> *Credit is a fantasy*
> *that always comes back to haunt you on payday.*

Financial Challenges Create Stress

Eighty percent of all visits to the doctor are stress related, according to the American Medical Association. Debt causes more stress than all other factors combined. The majority of divorces are due to financial stress. Like cancer, if not eliminated, debt will destroy you.

I was told about a 26-year-old who called her parents and asked for $125,000 to pay off her credit card debt. She was in trouble, way in over her head, actually. Her parents came to her rescue and paid them off. Two years later she called her parents again, now with $140,000 of credit card debts. Her parents chose to "save" her again and sold their home to do so. What an example of the possible consequences of not teaching your children to be independent!

Millions of college graduates, many married, are back living in their parents' basements for free room and board. This is primarily due to three reasons: credit card debt, student loan debt, and not being taught to be independent.

Many seniors retire in the red and spend more than 40% of their household income on debt payments. MSNBC.com reported, "The average credit card debt for consumers ages 65-69 skyrocketed more than 200% from 1992 to 2001. It now tips the scales at nearly $6,000, according to stats compiled for a recent national Consumer Law Center report."

Financial stress has many people choosing bankruptcy, which hurts everyone because it increases prices. It is shocking how many peoplee commit suicide due to all the pressure and sense of hopelessness.

Wanted—Your Money

Your job is to keep the money you earn, because people are working day and night thinking of ways to get as much of it as possible.

Every type of advertising, persuasion, guerrilla marketing, and scam tries to get you to take on one more monthly payment and go further in debt. *The Wall Street Journal* recently reported that many large national companies advertise the three "No's": no down payments, no interest, and no monthly payments for months or years. This is a lie. You will pay, one way or another.

Banks push a cashless society. When you are not conscious of the money you spend (you don't see money), you spend more and pay more interest.

There is only one way to beat the system, **stop using credit—pay cash!**

Are You a Long-Term Customer?

NBC News reported that in the first semester, college students receive offers from about 50 credit card companies. They receive credit cards based on their expected ability to repay. Credit card companies know that if their card is in the students' pockets, those people are more likely to be long-term customers. Most students end up with two to five credit cards, and no clue about how bad it can be for their financial health.

In 2004, 76% of all college undergraduates had credit cards with an average outstanding balance of $2,169. After graduation, instead of focusing on creating funds for their financial freedom, they have lots of debt and will spend years digging out of it.

Read Chapter 10 on financing college and you may not even need a credit card.

Do You Read the Fine Print?

Most people don't. *Bottom Line/Tomorrow*, February 2006 says, "Credit card companies now charge interest rates as **high as forty percent** a year. There's no legal limit on the amount they can charge—and, it seems, no limit to the tricky terms and conditions, hidden in the fine print, that card companies impose on unwary consumers." There are "elastic" contract terms that allow the credit card companies to change their terms for no reason. And there's more.

- Late fees average $34.
- A late payment can result in a drop of your credit score, up to 100 points. Your mortgage payment could increase $100 for just a drop of 50 points.
- Exceed the credit limit and a penalty interest rate of 30% or more may be assessed.
- Paying a credit card bill by phone can cost you $5-$15.
- If you pay online, it's usually free; and there can be a waiting period of up to 48 hours before it posts. One company allows an online payment only every five business days, which, if you're paying from several bank accounts, increases the amount of interest they earn.
- There are different interest rates, depending on the type of transaction—purchases, cash advances, transfers. Cash advances usually have the highest rate and are bank robbery in reverse.

- Some companies use a billing method that charges interest on debt already paid. For example, you begin with a zero balance and charge $1,000. You pay $990 on time, expecting to pay interest on only $10. Instead, you pay $15 interest on the full $1,000.
- At least one company will deactivate your card if you don't use it and you must then pay to reactivate the card.
- Beware of teaser interest rates of 1.9%, 2.9%, and 3.9%. Most teaser rates last only a few months, then the rate is shocking.
- The cash-back "rewards" sound great, yet the fine print may limit the $150 perceived reward to no more than $35-$40 per quarter. Or there may be no reward unless you keep a balance on the card. Is the ⅒ percent of money received worth the higher variable interest rate?

More Fine Print—The Universal Default Trap

Many credit card companies are just waiting for you to miss a payment. They've developed the concept of "universal default" to make it easier for them to jack up your interest rate. The universal default clause in your credit card agreement lets the company raise your interest rate even if you're late with a payment **to some other creditor**.

For instance, if you miss a car payment, or you're late on some other credit card, phone bill, or any utility bill, then your other credit cards' interest rates can shoot up—even though you've signed up for a zero-interest offer and have always paid that bill on time.

A universal default clause is becoming standard in credit card agreements; in fact, almost half of card issuers have one and enforce it. Your self-defense

Sample Universal Default Clause

"If cardholder is reported as delinquent on an account with any other creditor, we may increase the APR (annual percentage rate) on your account up."

is to read the fine print of your credit card agreement to see if you are subject to it.

No-Late-Fee Credit cards

Grace periods, the time in which a payment is not considered late, have historically been one month. Today those grace periods average just 23 days, making it easier for credit card companies to hit consumers with late fees. Sensing an opportunity, companies have developed no-late-fee credit cards. These cards often carry no annual fees and can save you as much as $39 for each late payment. Sounds great, and here are some of the traps:

- When you repeatedly miss the payment deadlines with some of these cards, your 0% introductory interest rate can skyrocket to 30% or more.
- Some companies eliminate the no-late-fee benefit during any billing period in which the customer doesn't use the card.
- If your payment arrives more than 30 days late, the card company will report your transgression to a credit-reporting agency, which could cause other lenders to raise rates on your outstanding debts.

Your self-defense is to steer clear of no-late-fee credit cards. Better yet, pay off all credit cards fast, then destroy them.

> *"The definition of insanity
> is doing the same thing over and over
> and expecting different results."*
> BENJAMIN FRANKLIN

The Absolute Best Way to Reduce Debt Is to Stop Creating It

You might choose to put into practice the following:

$ If you're addicted to buying, then stay away from temptation. It's amazing how you don't need something if you don't know it's on sale. Stay away from newspaper ads, TV ads, aimless wandering in the stores, and browsing the Internet for "deals."

$ Are you participating in retail therapy? Are you shopping to make yourself feel better, to feel loved, to be happy? If so, it usually lasts only a day or so and then you need another "fix." Record and acknowledge your feelings. Perhaps going for a walk with someone you care about would be more fun.

$ Calculate how much income you make an hour. Let's say it's $25. When you see the sweater for $90, ask yourself, "Is the sweater worth 3.6 hours of my precious time?"

$ Follow the 20/24 rule and take time out. For every $20 you plan to spend, wait 24 hours and ask yourself, "Do I really need this?"

$ Leave your checkbook and credit card at home. If you find something you want, put it on hold for 24 48 hours. If after you get home it becomes a need, you can always go back and purchase it.

$ Ask yourself before you hand over your money.
> ~ Is this a real need or just a want?
> ~ What will happen if I do not purchase it today?
> ~ Why didn't I need it three weeks ago?
> ~ Will I need it three months from now?
> ~ Will a less expensive item do just as well?

There will be 2 billion trips to the malls, just in December. Purchases are so robust and have been for so long that some retailers wonder if shoppers will hit the saturation point with no more room in their homes, closets, and garages.

$ Associate with people who support your saving and investing plan.

$ Most people wear only 20% of the clothing in their closet. Do you have clothing that has never been worn and still has the price tags attached? With every piece of clothing you consider bringing into your home, ask yourself,
> ~ Does it make me feel fabulous?
> ~ Does it make my top ten list of favorite things to wear?

If the answer is "no" to either question, leave the item where it is, even if it's free.

$ **Use a credit card** *only* **if you have the cash to back it up.**

Some final thoughts. If you do not change what you are doing (or spending) today, tomorrow will be the same as yesterday. You will continue helping make others millionaires instead of becoming one yourself.

Resources

Book

The Two-Income Trap:
  Why Middle-Class Mothers And Fathers Are Going Broke
  by Elizabeth Warren and Amelia Warren Tyagi

Web site

If you must have a credit card, compare carefully.
  bankrate.com

"This is not that rainy day."
DEBORA MANASSAS

| Chapter 8 | *How to Quickly*
Become Debt-Free |

You, like most people, want to enjoy the finer things in life. Take a cruise, go on expensive vacations, travel to far corners of the world, enjoy a lovely home, etc. This would be an ideal time to reread the story of *The Richest Man in Babylon*. In my opinion, the most fascinating paragraph in the story is:

> *"Arkad was famous for his wealth, kindness and generosity.*
> *He gave graciously to charities, was generous with his family,*
> *and liberal with his own expenses.*
> *Arkad was rich and generous,*
> *and each year his wealth increased faster than he spent it."*

Be honest, wouldn't you enjoy having all the good things in life and still have **your investments grow faster than you could spend them?**

The entire object of this book is to make this prospect a reality so that you can enjoy your wealth at the youngest age possible. Make a commitment now that you want to be like Arkad, wealthy while young.

I purchased a book entitled *How To Be Successful and Make Your Dreams Come True* and it had only six words, "Wake Up, Get Up, Get Going!" Best $6.95 investment I ever made.

To help you "Get Going," I am going to give you three alternative methods to become debt-free in two to five years. One method includes paying off your car and home. Choose the best way for your family and, then, follow it.

Remember, if you are interested in living the good life and becoming a multimillionaire, you will want to reduce your costs. See the Appendix for a list of *2000 Ways to Lower Living Expenses*.

Debt Lowers Your Standard of Living

Understand that debt lowers your standard of living every month. Every penny you pay in interest is less money that you have for you and your family! The average family pays almost $11,000 interest on credit per year, or $916 per month. Imagine what you could do with an extra $916 per month!

Everything you purchase delays your financial freedom, plus you have to find a place for it and clean it weekly. Avoid impulse buying or "malling." Credit takes more money away from you, keeping you from achieving your financial goals. We have been brainwashed into thinking that we cannot live without credit. This is a false, ruthless idea that will rob you blind. Do not be fooled.

IRS studies show that 96 out of 100 financial failures are caused by the **inability to delay gratification**. They bought on credit and gave their future away.

One couple, married 10 years, moved into a larger home because they had so much stuff: 10 computers, motorcycles, boat, RV, etc. They commuted and worked 13 hours a day, six days a week to earn more money to pay their increased mortgage payment. Sadly enough, they were too tired to use their things on their one day off.

Become a CIA Agent

Take a small notebook or index cards and track every penny and dollar you spend and what you spend it on for a week—just a week. Track all the cash you spend, the checks you write, the charges you put on your credit cards, and all automatic bills paid. At the end of the week, on another sheet of paper, list each expenditure under these headings: Necessity, Convenience, Indulgence, Appearance.

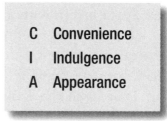

C Convenience

I Indulgence

A Appearance

How quickly would your debts be paid off with the money you are currently spending on Convenience, Indulgence, and Appearance?

Achieve the American Dream

You want the best for your family. So husband, wife, and children agree on the concept and details of getting out of debt.

Your family agrees:

$ That being debt-free will benefit the entire family

$ You will be one of the 30% of Americans who have the means to pay for what you need, when you need it, so you won't be living paycheck to paycheck

$ You will be one of the 4% who retire rich

$ That credit has short-term gain and long-term pain

$ You will practice delayed gratification

$ To spend money only on the necessities

$ That if you want things and more things, you will pay cash

$ To focus all available money on the bills until you are debt-free

$ To cut up the credit cards

Method One—Power Pay

The first method will be to pay off each debt one by one. Make a list of all the debt you owe, including your home.

Owed To	Total Amount Due	Monthly Payment
Credit card #1	$600	$100
Credit card #2	$1,600	$200
Credit card #3	$3,000	$300
Loan#1	$2,500	$250
Loan#2	$4,000	$275
Auto Loan	$13,000	$400
Mortgage	$60,000	$1,000

Remember!
You can DO what you want to do.
You can BE what you want to be.
You can ACHIEVE what you want to achieve.

Step 1

Implement this plan by paying off your **smallest** two debts first, regardless of interest rate. Having them paid off will give the entire family a positive psychological boost.

Sources of Funds to Pay Off Debt #1, $600

Regular monthly payment	$100
See Appendix for list of *2000 Ways to Lower Living Expenses*	
Reduce monthly spending	$100
Reduce monthly food costs	$100
Reduce monthly eating out	$100
Reduce monthly entertainment	$50
Reduce monthly utility costs	$50
(free analysis from each utility company)	
Reduced taxes taken out of paycheck	$100
Total monthly payment	**$600**

Payoff time is 1 month instead of 6 months.

Have a family celebration with a special dinner, paying cash of course, and burn a **copy** of the debt.

Step 2

Now pay off the second smallest debt, regardless of the interest rate. Again, it's for the psychological boost.

Sources of Funds to Pay Off Debt #2, $1,600

Regular monthly payment	$200
Money from first debt paid off	$600
Total monthly payment	**$800**

Payoff time is 2 months instead of 8 months.

Have another family celebration by going out to dinner, and burn a **copy** of the second debt. It is very important that this become a family celebration.

It takes guts to leave the ruts!

Step 3

Now it is **very important** to select the debt with the highest interest rate.

Sources of Funds to Pay Off Debt #3, $3,000

Regular monthly payment	$300
Money from first two debts paid off	$800
See Appendix for list of *2000 Ways to Lower Living Expenses*	
Additional cost reductions	$100
Total monthly payment	**$1,200**

Payoff time is 2.5 months instead of 10 months.

Remember, it's very important to have a family celebration and burn a **copy** of your third debt.

Step 4

Pay off the fourth debt with the next highest interest rate.

Sources of Funds to Pay Off Debt #4, $2,500

Regular monthly payment	$250
Money from first three debts now paid off	$1,200
Total monthly payment	**$1,450**

Payoff time is 2 months instead of 10 months.

> *Be prepared to pay the price for your financial freedom.*
> *It's worth it!*

Step 5

Pay off the fifth debt with the next highest interest rate.

Sources of Funds to Pay Off Debt #5, $4,000

Regular monthly payment	$275
Money from first four debts paid off	$1,450
Total monthly payment	**$1,725**

Payoff time is 2.5 months instead of 15 months.

Step 6

Congratulations! You are now paying your auto loan.

Sources of Funds to Pay Off Debt #6, $13,000

Regular monthly payment	$400
Money from first five debts paid off	$1,725
Total monthly payment	**$2,125**

Payoff time is just over 6.5 months instead of 32.5 months.

Look what you have accomplished! You have reached a major milestone. You have paid off all your debts in 15¾ months instead of 90 months. Now is the time for a really big celebration or vacation, paying cash of course! Remember to burn a **copy** of the car loan contract during your celebration.

Step 7

Now I want you to use the same efficiency of compounding by concentrating on your last debt—your home mortgage. This is the greatest fun of all. Assume your mortgage balance is $60,000 with a $1,000 monthly payment.

Sources of Funds to Pay Off Your Last Debt, #7, $60,000 mortgage

Monthly mortgage payment	$1,000
Money from first 6 debts paid off	$2,125
2nd $100 from W-4 changes	
Reduced taxes taken out of paycheck	$100
See Appendix for list of *2000 Ways to Lower Living Expenses*	
Reductions of expenses	$175
Total monthly payment	**$3,400**

Original Payoff, in months ($1,000/mo)	81
In years	6.75
Actual Payoff, in months	18
In years	1.5
Time Saved, in years	5.25

This family became 100% debt-free in less than three years and has 100% equity in their home, cars, furniture, etc. Tens of thousands of interest dollars were saved. Almost all families can be debt-free in two to five years. Once that's accomplished, **you are ready to become a millionaire quickly.**

Summary of Method One—Power Pay		
	ORIGINAL	ACTUAL
Number of debts	7	7
Payoff in months	171	33
Payoff in years	14.25	2.75
Time Saved 11.5 years!		

Funds Now Available for Investing

Now that you are free of debt, you are ready to build wealth quickly. Remember, you were paying $3,400 on your home per month. Now I want you to take that $3,400 and put it to work to quickly build wealth for you.

$3,400 invested monthly @ 15% compounded monthly

	TOTAL INVESTED	PRINCIPAL/INTEREST
10 years	$408,000	$947,435
15 years	$612,000	$2,301,335
20 years	$816,000	$5,154,247
25 years	$1,020,000	$11,165,851
30 years	$1,224,000	$23,833,390

The Power of Compounding working for you!

Method Two—Credit Consolidation

This applies to all your credit cards and loans only. The average household uses 14.2 credit cards. Just think of the **time, cost, stress**, and **loss of prime family time** given up each month to keep track and audit all those credit card statements.

For 20 years I have been teaching people in my seminars how to eliminate credit card debt and become wealthy while still young. The object is to consolidate all your credit cards into one credit card.

Here's the game plan:
- Pay cash for **all** your purchases, starting now.
- Make a list of your credit cards with six columns.
    - ~ Name of credit card
    - ~ Balance owed
    - ~ Current interest rate
    - ~ New rate offered
    - ~ Terms of the new rate
    - ~ Conditions of the new rate
- Rearrange the list beginning with the lowest interest to the highest interest rate.
- Call the credit card company with the **lowest interest rate** first and ask, "Would you be interested in my other balances being consolidated into your credit card?" Some companies will reward you with six months of free or reduced interest. Remember to find out what the interest rate will be after the six months are over.
- Repeat the process with the five lowest interest rates.
- Negotiate the best interest, terms, and conditions for each.
- Compare rates, terms, and conditions.
- Consolidate with the company that offers you the best deal.
- As you consolidate, cut up all other cards. Put the current card in a safe place, perhaps the freezer.
- Pay as much money on the card as you can every month. Make payments every other week if you can.
- Have a great family celebration when it is paid off!

- Decide to use the card ONLY if you have the cash in the bank AND you pay it in full each month.

Method Three—Use Your Home Mortgage

Another option would be to refinance your home mortgage with a low interest rate and pay off all credit cards and loans. Home mortgages have the lowest interest rate in American and the interest is 100% tax deductible.

A word of caution. Focus on paying cash for everything at this point. Cut up all but one credit card and use it only if there's cash to back it up. This is imperative!

Advantages of Being Debt-Free

$ Financial freedom for you and your family
$ 80% more after-tax dollars to spend how you choose
$ You will build savings and become your own banker, credit card company, etc., by investing the money that had been going to debt-elimination payments
$ Your home is paid for, free and clear
$ Your car(s) are paid for, free and clear
$ Many more options
$ You have cash on hand for anything
$ More peace, calmness, and enjoyment
   ~ More years to your life
   ~ Lower medical bills
   ~ A more romantic life
$ No credit card or installment loan payments
$ No boss can hold a job over your head
$ No possibility of bankruptcy or home foreclosure
$ No liabilities
$ Never have to worry about a credit rating
$ You will never need credit again

How to Quickly Build Wealth

You can live the good life on a cash basis and live like a king!

Building wealth requires that you plan ahead. Remember that it wasn't raining when Noah built the Ark. Plan ahead. **Focus all available funds on wealth creation.**

$ Former monthly credit card payments
$ Former car loans and/or lease payments
$ Former installment, personal loan, home mortgage payments
$ Raises and bonuses from work
$ Company pension, profit-sharing, or retirement plans
$ Income tax refunds (if any)
$ Spouse's income
$ Audit your bills before paying them. The average family spends $1,000 a year on incorrect and duplicate charges.
$ All other sources of income
$ Home-based business

Remember

$ You will never become wealthy if you pay credit card interest.
$ Use a credit card ONLY if you have the money in the bank AND you pay it in full each month.
$ The only interest anyone should ever pay is investment interest that is generally tax deductible.
$ Only four households out of 100 are ready for retirement. **Determine now to be one of the four** and be like Arkad, the richest man in Babylon.

Resources

Online calculator
    mindyourfinances.com/calculators/savings-calculator

Web site
    debtsteps.com/budgeting.html

What would your life be like if you had more money than you could spend like Arkad, the richest man in Babylon?

Chapter 9	*Become a Multimillionaire from Home Ownership*

Home ownership is a personal matter, with two major schools of thought.

First School of Thought

Pay off your mortgage as quickly as possible. The reasons: added security, no more monthly mortgage payments, your home is paid for if you become disabled, the list goes on and on.

Assume your home is worth $375,000 in today's market. If you have and/or want to have your home paid for in full with no monthly mortgage payments, there is a gigantically important question. "Would you leave $375,000 cash in $1,000 bills on your kitchen table when you leave the house today and every day thereafter 24/7 for 365 days a year, year after year?"

Of course not!

Second School of Thought

I have been teaching this for decades—become a multimillionaire from home ownership, whether it's paid for or not. Would you believe that when your home is paid for it is called a dead asset? Your home equity is dead and not working for you. Please memorize this saying.

> *Instead of working hard for my money*
> *I have my money working hard for me!*

This goes for your home equity as well. Investing your home equity is one of the easiest ways to become a multimillionaire. You say, "I do not want a mortgage on my home." "Why not? You're not giving up a penny." You automatically have the assets you invest in; it doesn't matter if the assets are in your home or some other good investment. Your home equity has not disappeared. You now have one or more off-setting assets to cover your home mortgage anytime you desire.

Interest-Only Mortgage
This plan applies to approximately one-third of you.

I do not want anyone to lose his or her home. This applies to those of you who have two or three sources of income so that you can maintain your interest-only monthly payments for up to two years in case of an emergency. For the rest of you, I hope that you can quickly get your financial house in order so you too can take advantage of this gigantic opportunity.

Take out an interest-only home mortgage for the largest amount possible, for the longest time possible, at the lowest fixed rate possible.

Call local banks. Start where you do your banking and/or where your current mortgage is. Also check the Internet for interest-only mortgages. Feel free to photocopy the next page for your use.

Now a number of banks are offering 40-year and 50-year mortgages, so ask for those rates. Why? Because the monthly mortgage payment may be lower than an interest-only loan. **Make sure the rate is fixed.**

There are four major items you want to accomplish:

$ You want the lowest monthly payment possible.
$ You want only the lowest fixed rate.
  Do not get involved with adjustable rates.
$ You want the longest term possible.
$ You want the largest loan possible.

All of the above is to lower your income taxes as you will see very shortly.

Here's an example of how an interest-only mortgage can make you a millionaire. Your totals may vary depending on your tax bracket, mortgage payment, and investment returns.

Locating The Best Interest-Only Home Mortgage

	1	2	3	4	5	6
Lender Name						
Do you have an interest-only mortgage?						
What is longest time possible?						
What is the best fixed interest-only rate?						
What is the 30-year fixed interest-only rate?						
What is the 20-year fixed interest-only rate?						
What is the 10-year fixed rate with renewable 10-year fixed?						
What is maximum loan on a $_____ home without holding insurance and taxes?						
Any other terms and conditions?						
Do you have fixed rate mortgage?						
What is the 40-year fixed rate?						
What is the 50-year fixed rate?						

Notes:

Instead of working hard for your money—have your money working hard for you!

$ Assume $300,000 interest-only home loan with 6% interest
 = $18,000 per year
 x 44.3% federal and state tax bracket
 = $8,000 tax savings per year

$8,000 invested yearly @ 15% compounded annually

	TOTAL INVESTED	PRINCIPAL/INTEREST
20 years	$160,000	$942,481
30 years	$240,000	$3,999,655

$ $500 average lower monthly payment for an interest-only mortgage. It is usually less expensive than a standard mortgage.

$500 invested monthly @ 15% compounded monthly

	TOTAL INVESTED	PRINCIPAL/INTEREST
20 years	$120,000	$757,977
30 years	$180,000	$3,504,910

$ U.S. Department of Labor figures show the average home in America doubles in value every 26 years. Obviously, in some areas of the country it will double much faster. For the sake of this discussion, let's say your home will double once in 30 years. The appreciation will be $360,000.

$ Results of 30 years interest-only home mortgage and appreciation.

Tax Savings	$3,999,655
Lower Monthly Payment	$3,504,910
Home Value Appreciation	$360,000
Total Profit	$7,864,565

You can **keep up this practice for life**. Almost every bank offers a 10-year interest-only mortgage. At the end of 10 years, most banks will allow you to renew by signing one form.

One person asked, "If you are paying only interest and no principal, where does the money come from to pay off the $300,000 mortgage loan 30 years from now?" Great question!

In 30 years you will have accumulated $7,864,565 from your investments, so sell $300,000 of your investments to pay off the $300,000 home mortgage loan and still have $7,564,565 left for you.

> Whether your home is paid for or not, in this example, you have $252,152 average income for the next 30 years. Keep repeating this and you have an income for life.

Advantages of an Interest-Only Mortgage
$ Lower monthly payments
$ Invest the difference from lower payments
$ Mortgage is the cheapest money available to borrow
$ Home values are not affected by having a mortgage
$ House doubles in value in 26 years
$ 100% of monthly payment will be tax deductible
$ Property taxes are tax deductible
$ Inflation working on your behalf in a remarkable, lucrative way

Simple Step-by-Step Procedure
- You have a home, paid for or not.
- If home is free and clear, take out an interest-only home mortgage loan for:
  - ~ The maximum amount possible
  - ~ At a fixed rate
  - ~ With the lowest possible monthly fixed payment
  - ~ Loan for as long as possible
  - ~ Read the fine print
  - ~ Repeat for life

  If only 10 years and a fixed rate, keep renewing until you die. Why? You might as well have and enjoy the extra income per year for your entire life.
- If you have a conventional existing mortgage on your home, replace it with an interest-only home mortgage with the same terms above.

- The great feature here is that your interest-only loan is 100% deductible on your income taxes. That means you now have $8,000 less tax to pay per year.
- You invest this $8,000 at the highest rate possible. You pay the monthly interest-only mortgage payment and keep the rest invested and compounding.
- Invest 100% of the average $500 lower monthly mortgage payment.
- In an emergency you could sell your home for double the original value and pay off the interest-only mortgage loan. Let's say the original home price of $375,000 doubles in 30 years to $750,000. Taking away the $300,000 loan paid off leaves you with $450,000 cash.

Remember, your totals could vary up or down depending on your federal and state tax bracket, mortgage payment, interest cost, and rate of return on your investments.

A few words about inflation would be in order. Inflation has averaged 4% per year since 1934. That means your interest-only home mortgage loan payments will cost you less in future months and years.

Another example. If you borrow $1,000,000 in today's dollars with 4% inflation, you would pay back only $401,007 in future dollars. Not bad: you borrow $1,000,000 and pay back just $401,007 over 30 years. This, my friend, is inflation working for you.

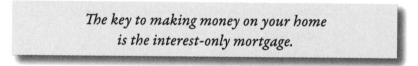

The key to making money on your home is the interest-only mortgage.

Second Way to Make Money from Your Home

If you do not want an interest-only mortgage, consider a home equity line-of-credit. I have had one since they came on the market in 1978. This is the best thing to happen since motherhood, apple pie, and baseball. Once you apply and get approved, you have a loan for life paying interest-only or any other outstanding balance you have when you like. The bank provides you with checks for your use for anything, anytime, no questions asked.

Generally, the banks will give you a home equity line-of-credit up to 80% of the appraised value. Take out the maximum loan and invest the money at a much higher interest rate. From your investment returns, you pay the interest and leave the rest invested to keep compounding or supplementing your income.

Third Way to Make Money from Your Home

The greatest gift Congress and the IRS have given Americans is to let us keep our own money (which was ours in the first place). Congress passed a law that allows tax-free profit from your home—single $250,000, married $500,000. You can quickly become a millionaire or multimillionaire by selling your appreciated home. You must have lived in it two years of the past five years. Remember, you can repeat this sequence every two years if you have good appreciation.

TAX-FREE profit invested one time @ 15% compounded annually

	$250,000	$500,000
	SINGLE PERSON	MARRIED COUPLE
10 years	$1,011,839	$2,022,778
20 years	$4,091,634	$8,183,268
30 years	$16,552,942	$33,105,885

Just think, this can provide you with an awesome income for life without costing you a penny.

Enjoy your free money!

Additional Ways to Make Money from Your Home

$ You can earn more than 200,000 free airline award miles when you buy, sell, finance, or refinance your home.

$ If your home is free and clear, take out a $100,000 interest-only mortgage. Purchase a $3 million life insurance policy with an annual interest-only cost of $3,000 per year.

$ You can take out a $1 million interest-only mortgage and create up to $20 million tax free for your favorite charity and heirs. See Chapter 20 for more details.

$ Please note, this is for seniors only. A reverse home mortgage allows you live in your own home as long as you like. Part of your homes equity is converted into tax-free cash with no monthly payments needed. The monies are paid back when the house is sold after you move out.

Resources

Free Airline Award Miles
   877-632-2200

Insurance Policies
   Allen Kaye and Associates, 800-662-5433

National Reverse Mortgage Lenders Association
   Free consumer guides
      866-264-4466
      reversemortgage.org/ConsumerGuides/tabid/251/Default.aspx

Online calculators
   mindyourfinances.com/calculators/savings-calculator
   fandktitle.com/calcs/allcalcs/invest_return_calculator.htm

Reverse Mortgage
   AARP, 800-209-9055
      Home Made Money brochure
         assets.aarp.org/www.aarp.org_/articles/revmort/
         homeMadeMoney.pdf

> *"All our dreams can come true—*
> *if we have the courage to pursue them."*
> WALT DISNEY

Chapter 10 | *College Can Be Free—for Parents*

Education is the best investment parents can teach their children. Education pays handsomely. According to the U.S. Census Bureau, the average annual salaries in 2004 were:

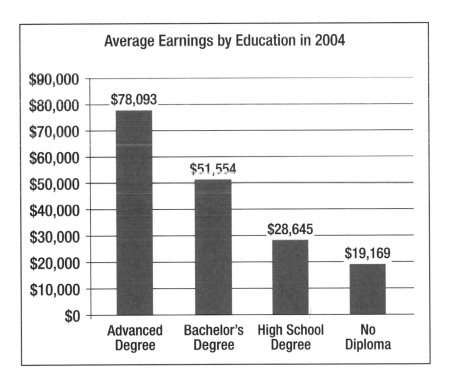

The difference in earning power between a person with a high school diploma and one with a bachelor's degree is $22,909 per year.

$22,909 invested yearly @ 15% compounded annually

	TOTAL INVESTED	PRINCIPAL/INTEREST
25 years	$572,725	$5,606,107
35 years	$801,815	$23,214,736

What would happen if you taught your children to be independent at a young age?

Too many parents today give their children virtually everything they want, even if the parents can't afford it. What they do not understand is—that by teaching their children to be dependent rather than independent—they are creating disabled children, youths, and adults. How many families do you know where the parents sacrificed financially for their children, and then didn't have enough money to retire comfortably? Or had to keep working and could not retire?

As parents you want, of course, to provide for and protect your children—it's instinctual and it feels good. Are you aware that there is a book that gives tips and tricks on how to get more money from your parents, even if you have to lie? Instead of being "the bank" for your children, be the "example."

Teach your children about money at an early age. Allow them to take risks and learn from their mistakes. Allow your children to become responsible with money. This is one of the best gifts you can give them.

Advantages of Teaching Children to Work

$ Teaches self-worth
$ Teaches character development
$ Teaches skill development
$ Teaches practical wisdom, known as "common sense"
$ Teaches habits of accuracy, courage, observation, diligence, and industry
$ Teaches economy and practical business management
$ Strengthens body and mind
$ Prepares them for independent living
$ Prepares them for a lifetime of business ownership or productive employment, and service
$ Instills dignity of labor

> $ Provides a financial benefit to the child, home, school, and nation
>
> $ Keeps them positively occupied

In my lifetime, I have found many fascinating surprises while working with high school and college age students.

- Children who learn and earn at an early age tend to be top leaders and contributors in their community and nation.
- The students who work their entire way through school
  - ~ appreciate their education far more than those who have everything paid for.
  - ~ usually earn better grades because they learn time management.
  - ~ generally have far more job offers at graduation.
  - ~ have higher starting wages.
  - ~ are promoted faster at their jobs.

All because of the eight years of full-time work in summers and part-time work during the school year starting as a freshman in high school.

Education Can and Should Be Free

By free, I mean free to the parents. The best education is the education the child earns himself. I can hear some saying, "All work and no play makes Johnny a dull boy." This would be true, if it were true.

My first job, after earning my master's degree, was chief dietitian at a college in Southern California. I also taught classes part-time and became acquainted with all the students.

Every student had 168 hours per week and it was how they used their time that made the difference. It was clear that the students who worked 20 hours a week, took a regular school load, and took time for play and school activities received better grades than the students who never worked. These students used time management and rarely gave the administration a hard time. The students who never worked, in contrast, were generally the troublemakers.

Funding My Education

My parents had 10 children, and times were tough during the Great Depression, with 25% unemployment and jobs scarce. And my parents taught us to enjoy work at an early age and still enjoy being a child with ample time for play.

By third grade, each of us was earning enough money to give to mother so she could purchase our clothes. In addition, we all earned 100% of our entire education from the third grade though college, some graduate school, and others medical school. Nine of the ten became professionals, including three doctors.

Students Earn While They Learn

Years later, one of my businesses operated the food service at a number of universities, colleges, boarding high schools, and hospitals. The presidents and principals told me to employ more students because they needed the jobs to pay their tuition. Because of the fixed contract, no way could we employ more students. The real problem was that the schools needed higher-paying, productive, piecework jobs on each campus. Almost a year went by with no resolution.

And I wondered, if my nine siblings and I could earn our tuition during the Great Depression, couldn't it be done again?

> *The best education is
> the education the students earn themselves.*

The principal and board of the largest school gave me permission to start an industry on campus and hire students. This was the beginning of a 10-year experiment to see if students could earn 100% of all school expenses for every year of their high school and college.

A full-time person was hired to visit businesses within 50 miles of the school. In spite of a bad recession, he succeeded in getting small, short-term contract work. To make a long story short, a full-time vice president was hired to run this new division. In four years there were 18 campus work centers in schools along the entire West Coast. We did packaging, assembling, collating, and light manufacturing of more than 200 products.

Word got around about the school who trained young people to earn while they learned (the school looked out over the Pacific Ocean, 60 miles south of San Francisco). One day a local newspaper reporter came to see for himself what was happening.

He was amazed at all the industries he saw, being operated by students with one or two adult supervisors. Industries included a large dairy farm, strawberry fields, kiwifruit vineyards, manufacturing of surf boards and solar panels, and the number one ultralight flying machine manufactured in the United States, called the Pterodactyl. (It was the only ultralight to fly from the Pacific Ocean cross-country to an air show in Wisconsin, then onto the beach in the state of Maine; no other ultralight had achieved this goal.) These were built by junior and senior high school students with adult supervision.

A TV news reporter from San Francisco happened to read the article and produced a one-hour documentary on the school, which was shown on Sunday night prime time. For the next two days the school's switchboard was lit up like a Christmas tree from business owners all around the Bay Area wanting to move their businesses to this special school. By now the school had 26 school industries and could not handle the 125 additional industries clamoring to get on campus.

Candles Create Jobs

One day I received a call at my headquarters in Southern California from a school in Oregon. There was a privately owned candle-making business on campus about to close. The school administration pleaded with me to buy the business because it employed 25 of their students. Against my better judgment, I broke down and four days and $25,000 later I was the "proud" owner of a candle business, knowing only one thing. It took 24 hours for other candle manufacturers to make a candle. The man I bought the business from was an outstanding inventor. He had created a 6-foot-long machine that took pieces of wax and using hydraulic power compressed the wax into a 3" or 4" wide x 6", 9", or 12" tall candle. **In just one minute a candle was made!**

One month after operation, the decision was made to pay the students piecework instead of $1.85 an hour, which was 60 cents over the $1.25 minimum wage. Within one month, the top 25% of the machine operators were making more than $12 an hour. Now remember, these were 17- and 18-year-olds. (Later I learned that the school administration hated me because some of the student workers made more money than the school principal!)

The candles were the first marbleized candles in the United States, and the highest-quality candle money could buy, and were produced 100% by high school students. They were smokeless, dripless, and burned 25 hours per inch. A 3" x 6" candle would burn 150 hours and these candles were in thousands of the finest stores in America.

As a result of my purchasing the candle company, four schools had industries where the students could earn their tuition. Two schools manufactured candles, another manufactured the beautiful wooden candleholders, and a university silk-screened the felt bases for the bottom of the holders. The university also made the pennants sold at every theme park and tourist attraction from the San Diego Zoo and Wild Life Park to Magic Mountain.

The businesses grew rapidly in only four months and—instead of losing the 25 jobs—several hundred were created. What a great joy it was to help students earn their own tuition!

Skateboards Worldwide

I will always remember when skateboards first became a national phenomenon. Art students at one of the universities where we had a large work center designed the winning design for our brand. Other students did the silk-screening. On the assembly lines, 100 students worked four-hour shifts, 24 hours a day to assemble the total skateboard. Overall, the work center employed 1,100 students.

It gave me fantastic pride to arrive at the largest campus work center location in an old abandoned gym at a university close to my headquarters. At 7 each morning, two to three long airline trailers were there to pick up all the skateboards completed in the previous 24 hours. They were packed in the airlines' half-circle shipping containers, which fit into perfectly fitting receptacles on the airline trailers. From the work center these trailers were loaded and off to Los Angeles International Airport and the skateboards were shipped around the world that same day.

Assemble and Package

At one boarding high school we had a large contract with a Fortune 100 company to assemble, package, shrink-wrap, and box 68 different bathroom fixtures. It made my heart expand in pride to see the 20-foot-long by four-foot-high displays in major hardware stores because I knew all those beautifully arranged quality products were assembled and packaged by 14- and 15-year-old students. I will put student workers up against older, more experienced employees anytime.

Many of the products assembled and manufactured were in many of the best stores in the world, including Macy's Fifth Avenue in New York and department stores in Tokyo, Japan.

The longest contract was for 28 years packaging fasteners, 2,400 different types of bolts, nuts, and washers. Students packaged the fasteners from bulk containers to 10 different size boxes ranging from a small matchbox size to a tissue-size box. When the students were paid an hourly rate, it took two and one-half days to package a 20-ton load with many mistakes. Within a week of going to piecework, the students packaged a 20-ton load in six and one-half hours with zero defects.

High Quality of Student Workers

It's very wrong for schools to pay their students minimum wage or slightly above. Next to health care costs, educational costs have increased above the inflation rate for years and are extremely high.

I recently had the privilege to speak to the entire student body at one of the top 100 outstanding schools as ranked annually by *U.S. News and World Report*. All of the 368 graduating seniors had jobs waiting for them (except those going to graduate school). The shocker was three began their careers the Monday after graduation with a $100,000 annual salary, plus 50% fringe benefits.

My point is this—what a disgrace on the part of a college or university to pay the students so little. All schools should have more piecework jobs, which pay well, so students can earn their entire way through school.

Good training, good supervisors, and piecework bring out the absolute best in student employees.

One thing I learned early: When you pay by the hour you only get one-half of the employee's production. Put the same employee on piecework and in less than two weeks, his or her production will double, and you will get zero defective work because the employees have to redo on their own time. Consequently, it is a win-win situation for all, from the student-worker making more money to the final consumer who receives a top-quality product.

It is great when the student can decide what he or she wants to earn versus the employer telling them what they will be paid.

During the 10-year pilot program, which ran into 15 years, 35,000 students were employed (from freshman in boarding high schools to college seniors) in 18 campus work centers. They earned up to 100% of all school expenses, including board, room, tuition, personal expenses, plus money left over in most cases.

After 15 years, my company, Versitron Industries, gave the schools all of the industries' capital improvements, equipment, and contracts as a gift—provided they kept the industries going.

Reduce Education Costs for Your Children

$ Parents, have your priorities straight. Your number one financial priority is saving and investing for your own enjoyment and early retirement. Allow your children to explore and benefit from the many opportunities available to them.

$ Teach children, at an early age, to be independent. It's the best gift parents can give their children.

$ With proper training most students should be able to earn their own tuition and they will graduate debt-free with few exceptions such as medical and dental degrees, etc.

$ If you own your own business, put your high school and college-age children on your board and pay them.

$ Grandparents spend a yearly average of $600 in toys for each grandchild the first four years of his or her life. Invest it instead, when the child is born, for college funds or leave it alone to grow even more.

$600 invested yearly for 4 years @ 15% compounded annually

VALUE AT	TOTAL INVESTED	PRINCIPAL/INTEREST
Age 18	$2,400	$24,376
Age 45	$2,400	$1,061,208
Age 65	$2,400	$17,368,307

$ Roth IRA

This is gigantically important for everyone, especially children. The IRS says children at age 7 and up can work and have earned income from their parents and others as they get older. **This means that children do not pay one penny tax if they earn $4,000 and invest it in a Roth IRA. If they do pay tax, it's at the "kiddie tax" rate.** A child can become a multimillionaire by age 60 by investing $4,000 a year in a Roth IRA from ages 12 to 18 ($28,000). The amount will grow to $18,033,781. Another great feature of the Roth IRA is that it is the only money you can pass onto the next generation without paying a penny in income tax.

$ Car upkeep is the next highest cost after tuition, room, and board. Have your children walk, bike, Rollerblade, or skateboard their way around town. Public transportation is also cost effective.

$ Purchase used textbooks direct from students when possible, then through the Internet.

$ There was an employment want ad in my newspaper for Costco Wholesale. They were hiring age 16 and up with starting wages at $10.50 per hour. Part- and full-time employees qualify for medical, dental, and 401(k). Your 16-year-old could work

> 20 hours a week during school @ $10.50/hour
> = $210/week x 39 weeks =$8,190, plus
> 40 hours a week in the summer
> = $420/week x 10 weeks = $4,200

Total annual wage for your 16-year-old would be $12,390. And this represents only one opportunity of thousands.

$ Cell phone—if the student has one, avoid text messaging because both parties are charged. Make phone calls during the free minutes. Communicate with friends and family by email, instant messaging, or use inexpensive/free Internet phone calling service.

$ Parents, be proud of your student's successes. Instead of paying $450,000 college expense for three children, invest that money for your early retirement.

$ Have your child graduate from college with great grades, great work experience, 100% debt-free with $313,493 return by age 22 and $15,835,473 by age 45. See next page.

Keep Your Money Growing

Never, never, touch your investment money until at least age 30 and even then keep most of your money compounding. Why? Like Arkad in *The Richest Man in Babylon,* you have to keep building your money tree until it is tall, large, and shady. Eventually your assets and investments will increase faster each year than you can spend the money. This is the point in life I would love for you to achieve, as young as possible.

Earn Your Entire Way Through College

$ Know the difference between your needs and wants. Learn save and invest from early childhood. The average teenager spends approximately $104 per week. Spend $50 and invest the rest for college.

$ Starting as a freshman in high school, work full-time in the summer, and 15-20 hours per week during the school year, and be debt-free at your college graduation.

$ Work for your parents in their business or profession.

$ Have a home-based business. Many financial experts recommend having one. It allows you to be able to take advantage of the tax laws for small business as well as create an income stream.

$ Take college classes during high school, and shorten the time needed in more expensive colleges.

Your Children's Investments

Young Child

Amount Invested	Total $ Invested	Principal & Interest at age 22	Principal & Interest at age 45
$500 one time at birth, BABY SHOWER	$500	$10,822	$269,385
$600/yr (age 1-4) TOY MONEY-GRANDPARENTS AVERAGE MONEY SPENT ON TOYS EACH YEAR	$2,400	$42,644	$1,061,208
$800/yr (age 1-5) 100% CHILD'S CASH GIFTS	$4,000	$66,752	$1,661,558
$1,000/yr (age 6-11) 75% CASH GIFTS, HIRE CHILD	$6,000	$46,836	$1,165,807
$4,000/yr (age 12-18) CHILD'S ROTH IRA	$28,000	$89,037	$2,216,252
$4,000/yr (age 15-18) CHILD'S EXTRA WAGES WAGES BEYOND ROTH IRA AND 75% CASH GIFTS	$16,000	$40,175	$1,000,006
$3,000/yr (age 19-22) CASH GIFTS, EXTRA WAGES DURING FOUR YEARS OF COLLEGE	$12,000	$17,227	$428,805
Investment Results	**$68,900**	**$313,493**	**$6,637,214**

Young Adult

Amount Invested	Total $ Invested	Principal & Interest at age 45
$8,000/yr (age 23-25) AFTER GRADUATION TO WEDDING	$24,000	$522,802
$15,000 Wedding Savings ASSUMES YOU MARRY AT 25	$15,000	$245,498
$9,375/yr Reduce Income Taxes AGE 25-45 (20 yrs)	$187,500	$1,104,470
$10,875/yr Interest not paid to others (20 yrs)	$217,500	$1,281,185
$26,000/yr Second Salary (6 yrs)	$156,000	$1,851,974
$100,000 from Interest-only Home Mortgage (20 yrs) LOW-END AVERAGE, PER YEAR	$0	$2,000,000
401(k) $1,250 per month (20 yrs) EMPLOYEE AND EMPLOYER CONTRIBUTION	$300,000	$1,889,888
Invest $100 twice monthly instead of $2,400 once a year from Income Tax Refund (20 yrs)	$48,000	$302,382
Investment Results	**$948,000**	**$9,198,259**

Principal and Interest at age 45	**$15,835,473**

$ Ask what discounts are available when paying cash.

$ There are many opportunities to do computer consulting.
The going rate in my area is $25 per hour for high school
age, $50 per hour for college students. Place ads at all the
senior retirement centers and in the local newspaper.

$ Attend a local junior college the first two years.
Make sure all credits will be accepted by the college
or university you will be graduating from. The cost is
minute in comparison to the top-ten universities or
private colleges. Your last two years attend an in-state
college at one-third the cost of a private college.

$ Do not pay mega bucks to get into the top-10 universities.
It is not the name, building, city, or faculty that make
the biggest difference. It is **your** ability to apply yourself
and learn from classes. And more important, the amount
of studying, extra reading, and research that makes the
difference. Having employed hundreds of professionals
in my life, I can say it is the student, not the school he
graduated from. Listen, there are many duds out there
who graduated from the top-10 and many shining star
employees who graduated from junior college and a
low-cost graduate college. Graduating from a top-10
university does not guarantee success.

$ Make an appointment with the college student finance officer
of your college of choice and apply for all the free grants,
scholarships, and every other type of free money available.

$ Consider a work/study college program.
Today you can earn more than $10,000 per year while
getting a college education and gaining tremendous work
experience in your field.

$ While at your college of choice visit the School of Business
to see if they sponsor a student business incubator, which
encourages students to start local businesses. It gives access
to and help from the professors in the School of Business so
the students can succeed.

$ Start your own business, hire other students, and sell it in your senior year.

One friend started a business as a college freshman. He earned more than enough to support his wife and two children, and pay his tuition. He graduated from college debt-free, sold his business, had $100,000 to invest, and had a job with a high-paying salary waiting for him. What a way to begin the rest of his life!

$100,000 invested one time @ 15% compounded annually

	TOTAL INVESTED	PRINCIPAL/INTEREST
20 years	$100,000	$1,636,654
30 years	$100,000	$6,621,177
40 years	$100,000	$26,786,355

If I were a student today, my first and foremost agenda would be to rent a small inexpensive space on or close to the campus and start a simple contract company. Provide outsourcing services where you can assemble, package, or do light manufacturing for businesses within 50-miles of the college. Employ dependable, sharp, students who can run circles around their counterparts around the world. Sell the business during the end of your senior year to a top freshman business major.

$ Purchase a business as a freshman and sell it at the end of your senior year.

I bought one my junior year and hired 75 part-time students from two local universities. The students earned more money then they ever had with the piecework wages and it gave me a great income. I sold the business after graduation for five times what I paid for it.

$ Get a waiter job in the nicest restaurant around.

The tips are better, giving you the most take-home pay.

$ Purchase a townhouse with three bedrooms and two baths. Rent two of the bedrooms to other students.

$ If you are going to be at a specific college for four years, purchase an apartment complex with your parents.

> You are paid to manage and receive free rent, there are good tax breaks, plus a good opportunity for appreciation. Naturally use leverage to purchase and apply for 100% financing.

$ Attend a college with "earn and learn" programs.

> There are a number of colleges where you can earn 100% of tuition, board, and room by working in one of their two to three dozen school industries. You commit to work 40 hours per week during the summer and 15 hours per week during the school year. You graduate from a top college debt-free with numerous job offers. My favorite is College of the Ozarks. You can work one or two days per month at Branson, Missouri, only two miles away for spending money. See Resources.

$ Sell this book to fellow students at your college or university.

> You will make good money while helping others become multimillionaires. See Resources.

$ Invest your party money

> In September 2001, *Money Magazine* stated the average amount spent by a full-time college student just on beer and pizza was $1,750 per school year. It is no doubt higher now.

$1,750 invested yearly for 4 years @ 15% compounded annually

	TOTAL INVESTED	PRINCIPAL/INTEREST
25 years	$7,000	$189,137
35 years	$7,000	$765,166
45 years	$7,000	$3,095,525

> *The quality of a person's life is in direct proportion to their commitment to excellence, regardless of their chosen field of endeavor.*
> VINCENT T. LOMBARDI

Zero Interest Student Loan

If you are a graduate student in medicine, dentistry, pharmacy, law, etc., a student loan may be necessary. It may not cost you a penny while you end up making money. If you borrow more than $60,000, the profit is even greater.

- Assume a $60,000 student loan for 30 years (the longer, the better)
- 3.42% interest rate per year (rate will vary)
- = $36,022 interest paid in 30 years (will vary) $100/month
- = equals $44.30 a month interest tax deduction at 44.3% federal and state tax rate (will vary)
- Invest the tax savings

$44.30 invested monthly @ 15% compounded monthly

	TOTAL INVESTED	PRINCIPAL/INTEREST
20 years	$10,632	$66,327
30 years	$15,948	$306,701

- In 30 years pay off $60,000 loan and keep $246,701 profit

Student Reward

I believe strongly in this educational philosophy. If your child has worked his/her own way through high school and college, I recommend you surprise the graduate with a new, moderately priced vehicle of his/her choice as a graduation present to show your appreciation and support for his/her achievement. This is a great help for a graduate to start his/her adult career and it will be highly appreciated.

Summary

$ Remember the best education is the education the students earn themselves.

$ There are many ways to get a college education for a fraction of the price of a four-year costly college or university.

$ There are thousands of ways to earn substantial income in high school and college.

$ It is 20 times easier for students to earn 100% of their educational costs than when my nine siblings and I did so many years ago.

Great success to parents and students as you embark on a great journey with awesome rewards.

Resources
Books
> *Dollars & Sense for Kids* by Janet Bodnar

> *How to be a Teenage Millionaire*
> by T.R. Adams, Rob Adams, Art Beroff, and Rob Adams

> *Seeds of Wealth* by Justin Ford
> A step-by-step program to help your children begin to build wealth and sound money habits from an early age.

> *Yes, You Can! Raise Financially Aware Kids* by Jack Jonathan, Sheelagh Manheim, Jim Stowers, Sam Goller, Alexis Preston

Earn 100% College Tuition
> College of the Ozarks, 417-334-6411

Online Calculators
> fandktitle.com/calcs/allcalcs/invest_return_calculator.htm
> mindyourfinances.com/calculators/savings-calculator

Sell this book and make money
> 800-310-5389   80ProvenWaysToBecomeAMillionaire.com

Websites
> *118 Ways to Save Money in College*
> scholarships-ar-us.org/student-living/save-money.htm
> *50 Best Values in Public Colleges*
> kiplinger.com/links/colleges06

> *Man's mind, once stretched by a new idea,*
> *never regains its orginal dimensions.*
> OLIVER WENDELL HOLMES

| Chapter 11 | *80 Ways to Become a Millionaire— Just Choose Two or Three* |

When Are You Rich?

When you can live comfortably, and securely, on income from your investments, you are rich. Until then, you are still in financial trouble.

I wonder where we Americans got the idea that we're all entitled to a retirement of leisure and financial security starting at age 65. Those are the rewards of becoming rich, not of becoming unemployed.

This is the appropriate time to review the main characteristics of a millionaire. What better place to go than the famous book *The Millionaire Next Door* by Thomas J. Stanley, Ph.D.? Any wonder why it was the number one business book after several years?

> *Remember your goal—To be wealthy while young, and worth $10 million in 20 years.*

Characteristics of a Millionaire

$ Lives well below income and invests the rest.
  Remember, if you expect to live a life of financial freedom, you need to have your money work hard for you.
$ Has goals.
$ Watches for bargains. Seldom pays retail.
$ Never buys on time; does not pay interest to others.
$ Eliminates unnecessary expenses.
$ Does not show off wealth.
$ Creates his/her own wealth—99% are self-made.
$ Does not pay unnecessary taxes.

> $ Pays his/her children salaries, not allowances.
> $ Does not tell kids that they are wealthy.
> $ Teaches his/her children to be financially self-sufficient.
> $ Manages time, energy, and money carefully.

Millionaires are not 10 times smarter, they just think differently. They focus on having their money work hard for them, rather than working hard for their money. You, too, can be a millionaire—even a multimillionaire and retire wealthy while young. Be like a postage stamp; it has the ability to stick to one thing until it reaches its destination.

$ Do not accrue any more debt
$ Pay off all debts fast
$ Operate on a 100% cash basis
$ Focus diligently on wealth creation and preservation, which is save and invest, save and invest, save and invest

"How can this be accomplished?" Read and follow this book; it will guide you on your journey toward wealth accumulation.

The rest of the chapter lists 80 ways to become a millionaire. Naturally, no one can accomplish the entire list. Neither do all apply to everyone. Just select two to three ways and incorporate them into your life. If you choose to add a new way every month, the good news is you can become a multimillionaire.

One day I was in Home Depot when a tall, handsome gentleman wearing a black suit, white shirt, and tie introduced himself. I had no recollection of ever seeing him before. He shared that he and his wife had attended one of my Wealth Creation seminars six weeks earlier and had learned a lot. They had wanted to see me afterward, and because most of the 1,700 attendees were in line to talk with me, they chose not to wait.

He said, "You told us to select two or three ways to become a millionaire." With a broad smile, he excitedly said, "This morning my wife and I started our **ninth** way to become a millionaire from your list."

I said, "You are not going to become a millionaire, you are going to become a multimillionaire." He was so pleased with their accomplishments in such a short time and that they were 100% focused on reaching their goal quickly.

Eighty Ways to Become a Millionaire
Choose only those that will be best for you and your family.

1. **Select the right mate**
   See Chapter 4 for details.

2. **Save on your wedding and invest**
   See Chapter 5 for details.

3. **Invest second salary**
   See Chapter 5 for details.

4. **Stop paying interest to others**
   See Chapter 5 for details.

5. **Use credit cards only if you have the cash**
   See Chapter 7 for details.

6. **Reduce your taxes**
   See Chapter 13 for details.

7. **Baby's growth estate**
   $500 from Baby Shower
   $500 from Parents
   $500 from four Grandparents ($2,000)
   When your baby is born, invest $3,000. See what a great
   financial foundation you have given your child!

   ### *$3,000 invested at birth @ 15% compounded annually*

VALUE AT	TOTAL INVESTED	PRINCIPAL/INTEREST
Age 18	$3,000	$37,126
Age 30	$3,000	$198,635
Age 40	$3,000	$803,590
Age 45	$3,000	$1,212,230
Age 50	$3,000	$3,250,972

8. **Parents eliminate tuition for private high school (4 years)**
    This is per child. See Chapter 10 for details.

    $10,000 invested yearly for 4 years @ 15% compounded annually

	TOTAL INVESTED	PRINCIPAL/INTEREST
20 years	$40,000	$537,352
30 years	$40,000	$2,173,889
40 years	$40,000	$8,794,592
50 years	$40,000	$35,579,029

9. **Transportation savings**
    AAA estimates the average yearly cost to own and operate a new, domestically produced, midsize vehicle was $8,410 in 2005. Depreciation (loss in vehicle value) accounted for $3,879 of that amount ($323 per month). Buy a creampuff, one-owner, used car and invest the depreciation savings.

    $323 invested monthly @ 15% compounded monthly

	TOTAL INVESTED	PRINCIPAL/INTEREST
20 years	$77,520	$489,653
30 years	$116,280	$2,264,172
40 years	$155,040	$10,143,413
50 years	$193,800	$45,128,923

10. **Home food purchases**
    The USDA reported the average cost of food prepared at home for a family of four in September 2006 was $6,337 for the thrifty plan, $8,088 for the low-cost plan, $10,068 for the moderate-cost plan, and $12,213 for the liberal plan. Increase your nutrition, eliminate food waste, and reduce your cost by $1,000 per year.

    $83 invested monthly @ 15% compounded monthly

	TOTAL INVESTED	PRINCIPAL/INTEREST
20 years	$19,920	$125,824
30 years	$29,880	$581,815
40 years	$39,840	$2,606,512
50 years	$49,800	$11,596,596

11. **Eat at home more**

    US Department of Labor reports that in 2004 the average family spent $2,434 eating out. Save by eating at home.

    Save 25%
    $608 invested yearly @ 15% compounded annually

	TOTAL INVESTED	PRINCIPAL/INTEREST
20 years	$12,160	$71,629
30 years	$18,240	$303,974
40 years	$24,320	$1,243,940
50 years	$30,400	$5,046,627

    Save 50%
    $1,217 invested yearly @ 15% compounded annually

	TOTAL INVESTED	PRINCIPAL/INTEREST
20 years	$24,340	$143,375
30 years	$36,510	$608,448
40 years	$48,680	$2,489,926
50 years	$60,850	$10,101,555

12. **Reduce income tax refund**

    The average yearly tax refund is $2,500. Instead of giving the IRS a free loan, add $2,400 back into your paycheck and invest your money. A $100 refund will avoid an underpayment penalty.

    $100 invested semi-monthly @ 15% compounded semi-monthly

	TOTAL INVESTED	PRINCIPAL/INTEREST
20 years	$48,000	$302,382
30 years	$72,000	$1,404,244
40 years	$96,000	$6,319,452
50 years	$120,000	$28,245,293

13. **Entertainment**
    U.S. Department of Labor reports the average family spent
    $2,218 for entertainment in 2004.
    Save 50%
    $1,109 invested yearly @ 15% compounded annually

	TOTAL INVESTED	PRINCIPAL/INTEREST
20 years	$22,180	$130,651
30 years	$33,270	$554,452
40 years	$44,360	$2,268,963
50 years	$55,540	$9,205,114

14. **Teen investment instead of spending**
    Teenage Research Unlimited reported that the average
    teenager spent $104 per week in 2003. Cut in half and invest
    the rest.
    Save 50%
    $52 invested weekly @ 15% compounded weekly

	TOTAL INVESTED	PRINCIPAL/INTEREST
20 years	$54,080	$343,552
30 years	$81,200	$1,602,368
40 years	$108,160	$7,243,991
50 years	$135,200	$32,527,990

15. **Save part of your vacation money**
    Stress is a health hazard. A break from the work routine is
    very important. Enjoy time with your loved ones, spend less,
    reduce your stress, and invest $2,000 per year.
    $2,000 invested yearly @ 15% compounded annually

	TOTAL INVESTED	PRINCIPAL/INTEREST
20 years	$40,000	$235,620
30 years	$60,000	$999,914
40 years	$80,000	$4,091,908
50 years	$100,000	$16,600,747

16. **At birth of each child**
    Parents and/or grandparents give a $2,500 one-time gift.
    ### *$2,500 invested once @ 15% compounded annually*

	TOTAL INVESTED	PRINCIPAL/INTEREST
20 years	$2,500	$40,916
30 years	$2,500	$165,529
40 years	$2,500	$669,658
50 years	$2,500	$2,709,143

17. **Contribute to your 401(k)**
    $15,000 a year ($625 twice a month).
    ### *$625 invested semimonthly @ 15% compounded semimonthly*

	TOTAL INVESTED	PRINCIPAL/INTEREST
20 years	$300,000	$1,889,888
30 years	$450,000	$8,776,530
40 years	$600,000	$39,496,576

18. **Your employer's 401(k) contribution on your behalf**
    Most employers have plans and match part or all.
    This is a 100% tax-free gift to you—Free Money!
    $5,000 per year ($416 per month).
    ### *$416 invested monthly @ 15% compounded monthly*

	TOTAL INVESTED	PRINCIPAL/INTEREST
20 years	$99,840	$630,637
30 years	$149,760	$2,916,085
40 years	$199,680	$13,063,962

    $7,500 per year ($625 per month).
    ### *$625 invested monthly @ 15% compounded monthly*

	TOTAL INVESTED	PRINCIPAL/INTEREST
20 years	$150,000	$947,472
30 years	$225,000	$4,381,138
40 years	$300,000	$19,627,347

19. **Roth IRA**
Double the amount for both husband and wife.
Triple the amount for husband, wife, and one child.
$4,000 invested yearly @ 15% compounded annually

	TOTAL INVESTED	PRINCIPAL/INTEREST
20 years	$80,000	$471,240
30 years	$120,000	$1,999,838
40 years	$160,000	$8,183,815

20. **Your child's Roth IRA**
The best time to invest! **100% tax-free.**

AGE	CONTRIBUTION	YEAR-END VALUE AT 15%
8	$500	$575
9	$750	$1,524
10	$1,000	$2,903
11	$1,250	$4,776
12	$1,500	$7,217
13	$1,750	$10,312
	$6,750	

$10,312 invested one time @ 15% compounded annually

VALUE AT	TOTAL INVESTED	PRINCIPAL/INTEREST
Age 40	$6,750	$448,936
Age 50	$6,750	$1,816,197
Age 60	$6,750	$7,347,531
Age 65	$6,750	$14,778,508

Consider this:
Instead of giving your children an allowance, hire them.
With earned income they are able to contribute a maximum
of $4,000 to their own Roth IRA.

If you are self-employed, in 2006 you were able to pay each
of your children $8,450. This can be deducted from your
business income, which reduces your own income tax,

Medicare tax, and potentially your Social Security tax. The children may pay zero tax after their standard deduction and IRA contribution.

If you are not self-employed, still hire your children and document it (give them a W-2). This way it's the type of income that qualifies for a Roth IRA. You could pay them at least $4,000 during the year.

Your child invests $4,000 a year while age 7-18 (11 years).

$4,000 invested yearly for 11 years @ 15% compounded annually

VALUE AT	TOTAL INVESTED	PRINCIPAL/INTEREST
Age 40	$44,000	$2,424,363
Age 50	$44,000	$9,807,901
Age 60	$44,000	$39,678,428
Age 65	$44,000	$79,807,492

21. **Refinance your home and save $100 per month**

$100 invested monthly @ 15% compounded monthly

	TOTAL INVESTED	PRINCIPAL/INTEREST
20 years	$24,000	$151,595
30 years	$36,000	$700,982
40 years	$48,000	$3,140,376
50 years	$60,000	$13,971,803

22. **Utilities**

U.S. Department of Labor reports the average family spent $2,927 for utilities in 2004. Free energy audits are available from either the utility companies or the city and save 25%.

$731 invested yearly @ 15% compounded annually

	TOTAL INVESTED	PRINCIPAL/INTEREST
20 years	$14,620	$86,119
30 years	$21,930	$365,469
40 years	$29,240	$1,495,592
50 years	$36,550	$6,067,573

23. **Invest only $50 a month**

    $50 invested monthly @ 15% compounded monthly

	TOTAL INVESTED	PRINCIPAL/INTEREST
20 years	$12,000	$75,798
30 years	$18,000	$350,491
40 years	$24,000	$1,570,188
50 years	$30,000	$6,985,901

24. **Eliminate recommended cash cushion**

    Have a home equity loan established for emergencies.
    You will have other assets, including stocks, where you can
    have your cash in two to four days.

    $25,000 invested once @ 15% compounded annually

	TOTAL INVESTED	PRINCIPAL/INTERESTD
20 years	$25,000	$409,163
30 years	$25,000	$1,655,294
40 years	$25,000	$6,696,588
50 years	$25,000	$27,091,436

    $50,000 invested once @ 15% compounded annually

	TOTAL INVESTED	PRINCIPAL/INTEREST
20 years	$50,000	$818,326
30 years	$50,000	$3,310,588
40 years	$50,000	$13,393,177
50 years	$50,000	$54,182,872

25. **Movies at the movie theater**

    The average general admission is $9. If you go once a week
    for a year that's $468.

    $468 invested yearly @ 15% compounded annually

	TOTAL INVESTED	PRINCIPAL/INTEREST
20 years	$9,360	$55,135
30 years	$14,040	$233,980
40 years	$18,720	$957,506
50 years	$23,400	$3,884,575

26. **Bottled water**
    The recommendation is to drink eight glasses of water a day,
    182.5 gallons a year. More people are drinking bottled water
    for health reasons, even though much bottled water has been
    found to be contaminated. The average price is $7.10 per
    gallon or $1,295.75 per year per person.

    Invest in a home water purification system, which will process
    1,320 gallons (approximately 25 gallons per week). The first
    year's cost is $0.46 per gallon. In the years to follow, with the
    purchase of a new filter, the cost drops to $0.13 per gallon.

    Drink healthy and invest your savings. The first year you
    will invest $685 (system is purchased) and then $1,120 the
    following years.

    ### $685 invested first year @ 15% compounded annually
    ### $1,120 invested yearly (2nd year on) @ 15% compounded annually

	TOTAL INVESTED	PRINCIPAL/INTEREST
20 years	$22,753	$124,831
30 years	$33,953	$531,164
40 years	$45,153	$2,175,006
50 years	$56,353	$8,825,263

27. **Soft drinks**
    The average person consumes 600 12-ounce servings per
    year, according to the National Soft Drink Association.
    That's 200 cans a month for a family of four, around $88.
    This does not take into consideration the increased health
    care costs. Drink water instead. It's healthier.

    ### $88 invested monthly @ 15% compounded monthly

	TOTAL INVESTED	PRINCIPAL/INTEREST
20 years	$21,120	$133,404
30 years	$31,380	$616,864
40 years	$42,240	$2,763,530
50 years	$52,800	$12,295,186

28. **Save on insurance policies**
 Rates are going down due to increased longevity. Any policy
 that is more than three years old may be replaced by one
 with the same coverage at a lower cost.

$500 invested yearly @ 15% compounded annually

	TOTAL INVESTED	PRINCIPAL/INTEREST
20 years	$10,000	$58,905
30 years	$15,000	$249,978
40 years	$20,000	$1,022,977
50 years	$25,000	$4,150,187

29. **Telephone bills reduced**
 There is no need to pay for long distance calls. There are
 companies with one flat rate for all calls. And the new Voice
 over Internet Protocol (VoIP) uses the Internet to make
 and receive phone calls. You can keep in touch easily and
 often. Also, millions of older people still unnecessarily pay a
 monthly rental fee for their phone instrument.

$600 invested yearly @ 15% compounded annually

	TOTAL INVESTED	PRINCIPAL/INTEREST
20 years	$12,000	$70,686
30 years	$18,000	$299,974
40 years	$24,000	$1,227,572
50 years	$30,000	$4,980,224

30. **The average cost of an engagement ring** in 2005 was
 $4,146. Save $2,000 and invest.

$2,000 invested once @ 15% compounded annually

	TOTAL INVESTED	PRINCIPAL/INTEREST
20 years	$2,000	$32,733
30 years	$2,000	$132,423
40 years	$2,000	$535,727
50 years	$2,000	$2,167,314

31. **Stop smoking**
    The average cost of a pack of cigarettes is $4.32, according to the Campaign for Tobacco-Free Kids. At one pack a day that's $30.24 per week.

    ### *$30.24 invested weekly @ 15% compounded weekly*

	TOTAL INVESTED	PRINCIPAL/INTEREST
20 years	$31,449	$199,789
30 years	$47,174	$931,839
40 years	$62,899	$4,212,659
50 years	$78,624	$18,916,277

    This does not include the money saved on extra mints or gum, teeth whitening, dry cleaning, life insurance, medical insurance, homeowners insurance, medical bills, and the additional cleaning needed when selling your home. Nor does it include the higher price given on auto trade-ins to non-smokers. Smoking can also affect your earnings–smokers earn 4%-11% less than nonsmokers.

32. **Omit 2-12 packs of beer a week**
    Average cost is $19.84 per week.

    ### *$19.84 invested weekly @ 15% compounded weekly*

	TOTAL INVESTED	PRINCIPAL/INTEREST
20 years	$20,633	$131,078
30 years	$30,950	$611,365
40 years	$41,267	$2,763,861
50 years	$51,584	$12,410,679

33. **Improve your lifestyle and reduce your medical expenses**

    ### *$3,000 invested yearly @ 15% compounded annually*

	TOTAL INVESTED	PRINCIPAL/INTEREST
20 years	$60,000	$353,430
30 years	$90,000	$1,499,871
40 years	$120,000	$6,137,862
50 years	$150,000	$24,901,121

34. Maintain a dog

The cost depends on its size and ranges from $780-$1,500. This example shows a medium-size with a life-span of 14 years. This is just for one dog, one time. What would the results be if multiplied by a number of dogs one might own in a lifetime?

$1,115 invested yearly for 14 years @ 15% compounded annually

	TOTAL INVESTED	PRINCIPAL/INTEREST
20 years	$15,610	$120,133
30 years	$15,610	$486,007
40 years	$15,610	$1,966,168
50 years	$15,610	$7,954,248

35. Maintain a cat

The cost is $640 per year. This example shows a lifespan of 14 years. This is for one cat, one time. What would the results be if multiplied by the number of cats one might own in a lifetime?

$640 invested yearly for 14 years@ 15% compounded annually

	TOTAL INVESTED	PRINCIPAL/INTEREST
20 years	$8,960	$68,955
30 years	$8,960	$278,960
40 years	$8,960	$1,128,549
50 years	$8,960	$4,565,610

36. Eliminate beer and pizza for college students

September 2001 *Money* magazine said the average amount spent by a full-time college student just on beer and pizza was $1,750 per year. It is no doubt higher now.

$1,750 invested yearly for 4 years @ 15% compounded annually

	TOTAL INVESTED	PRINCIPAL/INTEREST
20 years	$7,000	$94,035
30 years	$7,000	$380,423
40 years	$7,000	$1,539,023
50 years	$7,000	$6,226,206

37. **Eliminate gym/health club fee**
    Walking is the best exercise and is free. Or you could
    purchase a treadmill with a one-time cost.
    Save $40-$150 per month depending on location.

    ### $40 invested monthly @ 15% compounded monthly

	TOTAL INVESTED	PRINCIPAL/INTEREST
20 years	$9,600	$60,638
30 years	$14,400	$280,393
40 years	$19,200	$1,256,150
50 years	$24,000	$5,588,721

    ### $150 invested monthly @ 15% compounded monthly

	TOTAL INVESTED	PRINCIPAL/INTEREST
20 years	$36,000	$227,393
30 years	$54,000	$1,051,473
40 years	$72,000	$4,710,563
50 years	$90,000	$20,957,704

38. **Save ATM fees**

    ### $43 invested monthly @ 15% compounded monthly

	TOTAL INVESTED	PRINCIPAL/INTEREST
20 years	$10,320	$65,186
30 years	$15,480	$301,422
40 years	$20,640	$1,350,361
50 years	$25,800	$6,007,875

39. **Interest-only mortgage payment**
    Invest the tax savings of $8,000 per year. See Chapter 9.

    ### $8,000 invested yearly @ 15% compounded annually

	TOTAL INVESTED	PRINCIPAL/INTEREST
20 years	$160,000	$942,481
30 years	$240,000	$3,999,655
40 years	$320,000	$16,367,631
50 years	$400,000	$66,402,990

40. **High school prom**

    USA Today reports prom night can cost $400-$3,000. Have a memorable time for less and invest the savings.

    ### *$500 invested one time @ 15% compounded annually*

	TOTAL INVESTED	PRINCIPAL/INTEREST
20 years	$500	$8,138
30 years	$500	$33,105
40 years	$500	$133,931
50 years	$500	$541,828

    ### *$1,000 invested one time @ 15% compounded annually*

	TOTAL INVESTED	PRINCIPAL/INTEREST
20 years	$1,000	$16,366
30 years	$1,000	$66,211
40 years	$1,000	$267,863
50 years	$1,000	$1,083,657

41. **Downsize home**

    Invest tax-free profits of $250,000, $500,000 if married.

    ### *Tax-free profit invested one time @ 15% compounded annually*

	$250,000	$500,000
	SINGLE PERSON	MARRIED COUPLE
10 years	$1,011,839	$2,022,778
20 years	$4,091,634	$8,183,268
30 years	$16,552,942	$33,105,885
40 years	$66,965,886	$133,931,773
50 years	$270,914,360	$541,828,720

42. **Become a real estate investor**

    With no down payment, earn $100,000 to $1,000,000 per year. Even teenagers can do this. See Chapter 15.

43. **Purchase property tax liens**

    See Chapter 12.

44. **Life insurance on you and your spouse**
Sell unneeded life insurance policies to companies that will purchase and then invest the money.

45. **Finance factoring or accounts receivable**
See Chapter 12.

46. **Home equity line-of-credit**
Reinvest at higher rate.

47. **Tax savings from gas and oil investments**
See Chapter 14.

48. **If your home is free and clear**
Take out a mortgage of $100,000 and purchase a $3,000,000 life insurance policy with an annual interest cost of $3,000 per year. See Chapter 20.

49. **Maintain a good credit score**
Would you believe delinquent library book fines, unpaid parking tickets, unpaid property taxes, and being delinquent with one credit card company negatively affects your credit score with all credit agencies? This means you will pay a higher interest rate when you borrow money (if you can even borrow)—for a house, home-equity loan, or for other investments.

50. **Create up to $20 million tax-free for your heirs**
See Chapter 20.

51. **Give your estate away two or three times**
See Chapter 20.

52. **Your social security could be worth up to $2,000,000**
See Chapter 20.

53. **Self-employed 401(k)**
    Husband and wife each can put in $44,000 per year or total of $88,000. Invest at 15% compounded annually. In seven years the $616,000 invested is $1,119,060.

54. **Invest twice monthly versus yearly**
    Invest $200 twice a month. In 30 years it's $2,386,750. Invest $2,400 once a year. In 30 years it's $2,086,776. Just think, $299,974 free money! That's an average of $10,000 per year for those 30 years. And this can go on for life.

55. **Income and appreciating real estate**
    Purchase well-located, carefully selected income real estate. Ownership of real estate has made more millionaires than has any other type of investment.

56. **Home furnishings**
    Purchase high-quality new furniture direct from warehouse stores and save 40%-60%. For greater savings, purchase formerly leased home furnishings from companies that rent furnishings. Also check companies that stage houses for sale.

    $5,000 invested one time @ 15% compounded annually

	TOTAL INVESTED	PRINCIPAL/INTEREST
20 years	$5,000	$81,833
30 years	$5,000	$331,059
40 years	$5,000	$1,339,318
50 years	$5,000	$5,418,287

57. **Web-based trading**
    Business Week Corporation puts on a weekend training program that teaches you the business of Web-based trading including options, stock selection process, and much more. Independent auditors surveyed 1,000 individuals who took the two-day training and found a 20%-24% investment return based on one hour per week.

58. **Pack a lunch**

The average purchased lunch is $6, with a 50-week work year that's $125 per month.

$125 invested monthly @ 15% compounded monthly

	TOTAL INVESTED	PRINCIPAL/INTEREST
20 years	$30,000	$189,494
30 years	$45,000	$876,228
40 years	$60,000	$3,925,469

59. **Repair and sell run-down homes**

Purchase, repair, and sell two to three per year part-time and make $100,000 per year. In 10 years you'll have $1 million.

60. **Multiply $12,000 annual tax-free gift 100 times**

Purchase $1 million life insurance policy. See Chapter 20.

61. **Reduced house payment**

An interest-only mortgage reduces your payment an average of $500 a month. See Chapter 9.

$500 invested monthly @ 15% compounded monthly

	TOTAL INVESTED	PRINCIPAL/INTEREST
20 years	$120,000	$757,977
30 years	$180,000	$3,604,910

62. **Dry cleaning**

Some sweaters can be safely hand-washed in cold water. Air your garments before hanging in the closet. Remove dust and lint with a clothes brush. Use a home dry clean product part of the time and save $50 a month.

$50 invested monthly @ 15% compounded monthly

	TOTAL INVESTED	PRINCIPAL/INTEREST
20 years	$12,000	$75,798
30 years	$18,000	$350,491
40 years	$24,000	$1,570,188
50 years	$30,000	$6,985,901

63. Save college tuition
     See Chapter 10.
     $25,000 invested yearly for 4 years @ 15% compounded annually

	TOTAL INVESTED	PRINCIPAL/INTEREST
20 years	$100,000	$1,343,380
30 years	$100,000	$5,434,722
40 years	$100,000	$21,986,480
50 years	$100,000	$88,947,574

64. Daily cup of cappuccino
     At $3.50 a day that's $105 per month.
     $105 invested monthly @ 15% compounded monthly

	TOTAL INVESTED	PRINCIPAL/INTEREST
20 years	$25,200	$159,175
30 years	$37,800	$736,031
40 years	$50,400	$3,297,394
50 years	$63,000	$14,670,393

65. Clothing purchases
     Spend less and invest the savings.
     $80 invested monthly @ 15% compounded monthly

	TOTAL INVESTED	PRINCIPAL/INTEREST
20 years	$19,200	$121,276
30 years	$28,800	$560,786
40 years	$38,400	$2,512,300
50 years	$48,000	$11,177,442

66. Manicure and pedicure
     Have once a month instead of twice and save $35.
     $35 invested monthly @ 15% compounded monthly

	TOTAL INVESTED	PRINCIPAL/INTEREST
20 years	$8,400	$53,058
30 years	$12,600	$245,344
40 years	$16,800	$1,099,131
50 years	$21,000	$4,890,131

67. **Text messaging**
Costs for both incoming and outgoing messages keep
escalating for this habit. What if you invested just $25?

$25 invested monthly @ 15% compounded monthly

	TOTAL INVESTED	PRINCIPAL/INTEREST
20 years	$6,000	$37,899
30 years	$9,000	$175,246
40 years	$12,000	$785,094
50 years	$15,000	$3,492,951

68. **Time is the most important component of investing**
Parents, invest only $500 at your baby's birth.

$500 invested once @ 15% compounded annually

	TOTAL INVESTED	PRINCIPAL/INTEREST
20 years	$500	$8,183
30 years	$500	$33,105
40 years	$500	$133,931
50 years	$500	$541,828

69. **Invest available funds once you become debt-free**
See Chapter 8.

70. **Toys for grandchildren**
Grandparents spend an average of $600 a year for the first four
years on toys for each grandchild. What a legacy if one or both
sets of grandparents would invest that money instead.

$600 invested yearly for 4 years @ 15% compounded annually

	TOTAL INVESTED	PRINCIPAL/INTEREST
20 years	$2,400	$32,237
30 years	$2,400	$130,417
40 years	$2,400	$527,608
50 years	$2,400	$2,134,469

71. **Purchase property trust deeds at a discount**
See Chapter 12.

72. **Instead of paying death taxes**
    Invest for heirs and favorite charities.

    ### Invest one time @ 15% compounded annually

	$100,000	$500,000
10 years	$404,555	$2,022,778
20 years	$1,636,653	$8,183,268
30 years	$6,621,177	$33,105,885
40 years	$26,586,354	$133,931,773

73. **Eliminate plastic surgery**
    Invest the savings and become a millionaire.

74. **Power of time and compound interest**
    Strive for the highest interest possible for life. See Chapter 2.

    Rule of 72
    Divide 72 by the interest rate to estimate the number of years it will take for money to double. See the difference earned at 4%, 6% and 15% returns.

4%		**6%**		**15%**	
Doubles in 18 years		**Doubles in 12 years**		**Doubles in 4.8 years**	
AGE		AGE		AGE	
29	$10,000	29	$10,000	29.0	$10,000
47	$20,000	41	$20,000	33.8	$20,000
65	$40,000	53	$40,000	38.6	$40,000
		65	$80,000	43.4	$80,000
				48.2	$160,000
				53.0	$320,000
				57.8	$640,000
				62.6	$1,280,000
				67.4	$2,560,000
Doubled 2 times		**Doubled 3 times**		**Doubled 8 times**	

If you were to invest at birth instead of 29, at 65 it would

Double 3.6 times	Double 5.4 times	Double 13.5 times

75. **Become a millionaire by getting an education**
    See Chapter 10 for details.

76. **DVD purchases**
    Monthly average purchases $50-$100. Save $25 and invest.
    $25 invested monthly @ 15% compounded monthly

	TOTAL INVESTED	PRINCIPAL/INTEREST
20 years	$6,000	$37,899
30 years	$9,000	$175,246
40 years	$12,000	$785,094
50 years	$15,000	$3,492,951

77. **MP3 downloads**
    The average album costs $9.99, songs $.99.
    $20 invested monthly @ 15% compounded monthly

	TOTAL INVESTED	PRINCIPAL/INTEREST
20 years	$4,800	$30,319
30 years	$7,200	$140,196
40 years	$9,600	$628,075
50 years	$12,000	$2,794,361

78. **Video games**
    The average video game player owns 60-80 games. The
    average spent on games each month is $83.
    $40 invested monthly @ 15% compounded monthly

	TOTAL INVESTED	PRINCIPAL/INTEREST
20 years	$9,600	$60,638
30 years	$14,400	$280,393
40 years	$19,200	$1,256,150
50 years	$24,000	$5,588,721

79. **Carefully managed family business**
    One family invested $250 to start a family business and it
    sold for $500 million 25 years later.

Investment Results at an Annual Rate of 15%

Invest Each Month	Total $ Invested	Principal & Interest 10 yrs	Total $ Invested	Principal & Interest 15 yrs	Total $ Invested	Principal & Interest 20 yrs	Total $ Invested	Principal & Interest 25 yrs	Total $ Invested	Principal & Interest 30 yrs
$10	$1,200	$2,630	$1,800	$6,164	$2,400	$13,271	$3,000	$27,566	$3,600	$56,318
$15	$1,800	$3,945	$2,700	$9,245	$3,600	$19,906	$4,500	$41,348	$5,400	$84,477
$20	$2,400	$5,260	$3,600	$12,327	$4,800	$26,541	$6,000	$55,131	$7,200	$112,635
$25	$3,000	$6,575	$4,500	$15,409	$6,000	$33,177	$7,500	$68,914	$9,000	$140,794
$50	$6,000	$13,151	$9,000	$30,818	$12,000	$66,354	$15,000	$137,828	$18,000	$281,589
$75	$9,000	$19,726	$13,500	$46,227	$18,000	$99,531	$22,500	$206,742	$27,000	$422,383
$100	$12,000	$26,302	$18,000	$61,637	$24,000	$132,707	$30,000	$275,656	$36,000	$563,177
$200	$24,000	$52,604	$36,000	$123,273	$48,000	$265,415	$60,000	$551,312	$72,000	$1,126,354
$300	$36,000	$78,905	$54,000	$184,910	$72,000	$398,122	$90,000	$826,968	$108,000	$1,689,531
$400	$48,000	$105,207	$72,000	$246,546	$96,000	$530,829	$120,000	$1,102,624	$144,000	$2,252,708
$500	$60,000	$131,509	$90,000	$308,183	$120,000	$663,537	$150,000	$1,378,280	$180,000	$2,815,885
$1,000	$120,000	$263,018	$180,000	$616,366	$240,000	$1,327,073	$300,000	$2,756,561	$360,000	$5,631,770
$2,000	$240,000	$526,036	$360,000	$1,232,731	$480,000	$2,654,147	$600,000	$5,513,122	$720,000	$11,263,541
$3,000	$360,000	$789,055	$540,000	$1,849,097	$720,000	$3,981,220	$900,000	$8,269,682	$1,080,000	$16,895,311

Invest Each Month	Total $ Invested	Principal & Interest 35 yrs	Total $ Invested	Principal & Interest 40 yrs	Total $ Invested	Principal & Interest 45 yrs	Total $ Invested	Principal & Interest 50 yrs
$10	$4,200	$114,148	$4,800	$230,467	$5,400	$464,424	$6,000	$934,997
$15	$6,300	$171,223	$7,200	$345,700	$8,100	$695,636	$9,000	$1,402,495
$20	$8,400	$228,297	$9,600	$460,933	$10,800	$923,849	$12,000	$1,869,993
$25	$10,500	$285,371	$12,000	$576,167	$13,500	$1,161,061	$15,000	$2,337,491
$50	$21,000	$570,742	$24,000	$1,152,334	$27,000	$2,322,121	$30,000	$4,674,983
$75	$31,500	$856,113	$36,000	$1,728,500	$40,500	$3,483,182	$45,000	$7,012,474
$100	$42,000	$1,141,484	$48,000	$2,304,667	$54,000	$4,644,243	$60,000	$9,349,965
$200	$84,000	$2,282,969	$96,000	$4,609,334	$108,000	$9,288,486	$120,000	$18,699,931
$300	$126,000	$3,424,453	$144,000	$6,914,001	$132,000	$13,932,729	$180,000	$28,049,896
$400	$168,000	$4,565,938	$192,000	$9,213,668	$216,000	$18,576,971	$240,000	$37,399,862
$500	$210,000	$5,707,422	$240,000	$11,523,335	$270,000	$23,221,214	$300,000	$46,749,827
$1,000	$420,000	$11,414,844	$480,000	$23,046,671	$540,000	$46,422,428	$600,000	$93,499,654
$2,000	$840,000	$22,829,688	$960,000	$46,093,341	$1,080,000	$92,884,857	$1,200,000	$186,999,309
$3,000	$1,260,000	$34,244,532	$1,440,000	$69,140,012	$1,620,000	$139,327,285	$1,800,000	$280,498,963

The purpose of all examples in this book is to encourage you to begin investing.
The calculations are from an interactive online calculator and are not intended to provide investment advice.

80. **Snacks**

One candy bar or soda from a vending machine a day is $30 a month. Two bags of chips a week is $24 a month.

$30 invested monthly @ 15% compounded monthly

	TOTAL INVESTED	PRINCIPAL/INTEREST
20 years	$7,200	$45,479
30 years	$10,800	$210,295
40 years	$14,400	$942,113
50 years	$18,000	$4,191,541

$24 invested monthly @ 15% compounded monthly

	TOTAL INVESTED	PRINCIPAL/INTEREST
20 years	$5,760	$36,383
30 years	$8,640	$168,236
40 years	$11,520	$753,690
50 years	$14,400	$3,353,233

Resources

Annual pay life insurance
    Barry Kaye and Associates, 800-662-5433
    Western Grant Group, 800-423-4890

Business Week Corporation
    800-724-25250

Online calculators
    mindyourfinances.com/calculators/savings-calculator
    fandktitle.com/calcs/allcalcs/invest_return_calculator.htm
    finance.cch.com/sohoApplets/CompoundInterest.asp
    bygpub.com/finance/InterestCalc.htm

Water purification system
    888-858-4221

Arkad kept one-tenth of all he earned and invested wisely. You, too, can do the same!

Chapter 12 | *How to Average 15% per Year on All Your Investments*

I taught for years that everyone should earn 15% or more average annual return on all their investments, including real estate. Now, some people roll their eyes and say, "Impossible." Well if it's "impossible," how then have I been able to do just that for the past 50 years?

First of all, I believed it was possible and I expected it to happen. Very powerful—one's beliefs and expectations. What do you believe? And what do you expect?

Secondly, many stocks have had 15% annual returns or higher. For example, the Small Stock Index has had returns of 15.7% for the past 50 years. The nice thing is you don't need to know anything about investing other than to be able to write a check to the discount broker marked "Small Cap Fund." That's it. Very easy!

Lehman Brothers' 10 most uncommon stock averaged 14% for the past 57 years. The Micro Cap Stock Index Fund averaged 13% for 80 years. So with a little knowledge and effort, one could easily reach the 15% average annual goal.

You could build your wealth the old-fashioned way, purchase stock in the most profitable asset class in the past century—plain old timber. From 1973-2002, timber produced an average annual return of 15% (1973-1981 returns averaged 22%). The demand for lumber keeps rising while the supply holds steady. The best way to invest in timber is Plum Creek Timber, a REIT that invests solely in timberland. And it's currently paying a dividend.

You do not have to be wealthy to learn how to invest and end up—as quickly as possible—a millionaire or multimillionaire. Invest $1 a week and increase it weekly as you apply tips from *2000 Ways to Lower Living Expenses* in the Appendix. As you become debt-free, you can invest even more!

Key Factors for Rapid Financial Success

These are my keys to being able to average 15% per year for 50 years.

$ Whom you marry is 80% cause for your success.

$ Marry the one you cannot live without, not the one you think you can live with.

> Make sure you are together on love-intimacy and financial-intimacy. It's the best formula for financial success.

$ Live on one salary and invest the second for at least the first six years of your marriage.

$ Follow Warren Buffett's plan.

> Almost 100% of his security investments were in stocks. Why? A major advantage is there are no taxes on stock appreciation until you sell, unlike mutual funds, which generally have higher commissions and you pay taxes every year. You pay tax if you keep the mutual fund or if you sell it, even if there was a loss.

$ Use leverage, which gigantically increases the rate of one becoming wealthy.

> Definition of leverage: "The use of credit or borrowed funds to improve one's speculative capacity and increase the rate of return from an investment." Financial leverage uses OPM (other people's money) as in the banks.

$ Do not pay interest on anything except your interest-only home mortgage and other investments that become income tax deductible, thus giving you more cash to invest.

$ No instant gratification.

> Everything you buy except consumables such as food, you have to find a place to put it in your house, garage, or yard. You have to clean it and maintain it until it breaks and gets thrown out.

$ Pay minimum income tax and invest the money for yourself.

$ Raise financially independent children.

$ Convert ordinary income (salary/wages) into securities and real estate. If self-employed, work out of your home and save taxes.

I have **averaged** 15% per year on all my investments for 50 years. Notice the word average. One can have an average gain of 75% one year and have zero gain the next four years and the yearly average would still be 15%. Do not be discouraged if some years your investments fall under 15%.

Another major factor to remember: Keep your good investments until you die. Do not listen to the voices telling pre-retirees to place more investments in bonds and other lower yield investments as they become older. Listen, it costs more to live in retirement than any other time of your life. Consequently, keep your great investments until you die.

Because you are reading this chapter, you no doubt want to know how people achieve a 15% return. You ask, "Who earns 15% ongoing?"

I have done this for 50 years. Did you know that there are hundreds of thousands that do the same or better? Watch the nightly business news and see one or more stocks that went up 15%-75% in one day. Each year, in the January 2 issue of *The Wall Street Journal,* or other major newspapers, you will find an annual report of all the 15,000 stocks and 14,000 mutual funds giving the total yield of each for the year. Some large newspapers have the stock appreciation for the year on a daily basis. It is fascinating to see how many grew 100% in the year. So be at ease, 15% is a reality for you.

Anne Scheiber's Legacy

Anne Scheiber's story is a legend that bears repeating. It will encourage you because, with the information from this book under your belt, you will be miles ahead of Anne Scheiber's knowledge of investing.

Anne Scheiber never earned more than $3,150 a year and yet in 1944 she invested $5,000 in stock. From 1944 to 1995 (when she passed away), she averaged 17.5% annual return for 51 consecutive years. She left $22 million to a New York City university to help needy girls receive an education.

What did she invest in because she had no, or little, financial knowledge?

$ Invested in leading brands
$ Favored firms with growing earnings
$ Capitalized on her interests
$ Invested in small bites
$ Reinvested the dividends
$ Never sold a stock she believed in

$ Kept informed
$ Gave something back

The one thing she could have done differently was to enjoy her money along the way. She lived like a pauper. You can choose to do it differently!

Great Investors to Date

Before I give you my list of favorite investments, here are three top professional investors of the past 100 years, and Anne Scheiber, a single lady. Interesting enough, she had no financial experience or investment know-how, and see how well she did. You can, too, if you choose to.

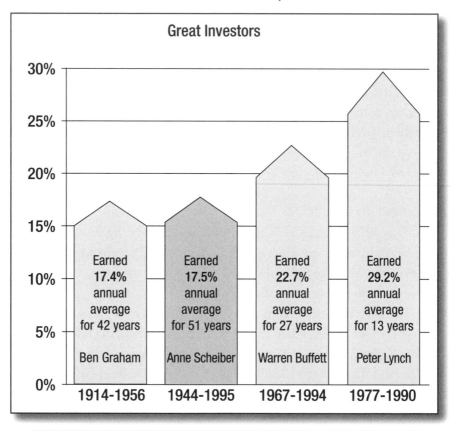

Great Investors

Earned **17.4%** annual average for 42 years	Earned **17.5%** annual average for 51 years	Earned **22.7%** annual average for 27 years	Earned **29.2%** annual average for 13 years
Ben Graham	Anne Scheiber	Warren Buffett	Peter Lynch
1914-1956	1944-1995	1967-1994	1977-1990

I never attempt to make money on the stock market.
I buy on the assumption that they could close the market
the next day and not reopen it for five years.
WARREN BUFFETT

High-Yield Investments

Company or Investment	Avg Annual % Return	Number of Years
• Interest-only home mortgage	$100,000 to $300,000 per year	Life
• Marry the one you cannot live without, 80% of all success depends on whom you marry. Make sure you have both love-intimacy and financial-intimacy.	Infinity	Entire Married Life
• Marketable trade, skill, or profession prior to marriage, if at all possible	$25,000 to $200,000	Working Years
• Eliminate credit card debt and invest for yourself.	145%	Life of Credit Card Use
• 401(k) for self-employed	$88,000 per Year	Working Years
• 401(k) as employee	100%	Working Years
• Other pension plans	50%-200%	Working Years
• Purchasing first and second mortgage trust deeds	15%-20%	Life
• Purchasing trust deeds at a discount	20%-50%	Life
• Factoring/Accounts Receivable financing	20%-40%	Life
• Venture capital companies	15%-40%	Life

Rates shown are no guarantee of future performance.

Company or Investment	Avg Annual % Return	Number of Years
• Tax lien certificates Guaranteed by the government. In use since 1698. 100% safe. Currently 5013 US counties have tax lien certificates to sell.	16%-50%	Life
• Watch your local newspaper financial classifieds for secured money to loan.	Varies 12%-30%	Ongoing
• Construction loans	Expect 15%-20%	Ongoing
• Reduce income taxes paid	15%	Ongoing For life
• Micro Cap Stocks	13%	80 years
• Stock Market	11%	71 years
• Investment Company of America	13.5%	64 years
• Lehman Brothers Brokerage Top 10 uncommon stocks	14%	57 years
• Small stock index	15.7%	50 years
• S & P 500	12.5%	50 years
• Acorn Fund (small companies)	16.3%	33 years
• CGM Capital Development	17%	30 years
• Templeton Growth Fund	15.1%	30 years

Rates shown are no guarantee of future performance.

COMPANY OR INVESTMENT	AVG ANNUAL % RETURN	NUMBER OF YEARS
• No-Load Fund	18%	26 years
	78%	last 5 years
• Dividend paying stock	15.2%	25 years
• Canadian General Investment, Limited (CGI)	15.2%	25 years
• Growth Fund of America	14.2%	24 years
• Gotham Capital, small hedge fund	40%	21 years
• Federal Realty Investment Trust 38 years of increased dividends	14.3% 30%	20 years past 5 years
• Mercury Insurance Group	16%	20 years
• Aqua America (largest water utility in US)	18%	20 years
• Columbia Acron Z#	15%	20 years
• Pacific Advisors Small Cap A	39%	20 years
• Berkshire Hathaway	17.3%	20 years
• Microsoft	22.4%	20 years
• Wells Fargo Bank, increased dividends	20%	18 years
• Dow, 10 highest dividend-paying stocks (adjusts each January 1)	20%	16 years
• The Prudent Specular	27.8%	15 years

Rates shown are no guarantee of future performance.

COMPANY OR INVESTMENT	AVG ANNUAL % RETURN	NUMBER OF YEARS
• Vanguard Health Care Fund	21%	15 years
• Smith Barney, aggressive growth A	18%	15 years
• FPA Capital Fund	18%	15 years
• Mairs and Powers Growth Fund	17%	15 years
• Sequoia Fund	16%	15 years
• Meridian Growth Fund	15%	15 years
• Muhlenkamp Fund	16%	15 years
• Contrafund	16.4%	15 years
• Enerplus Resources (gas and oil)	47.3%	14 years
• Ariel Mutual Fund - Ariel Fund	14%	12 years
• Alleta (energy services in upper Midwest, including electric, gas, and water)	18%	10 years
• Corporate Office Properties Trust Real Estate Investment Trust (REIT)	29%	10 years
• Fidelity-leveraged company stock fund	23.42%	10 years
• Fidelity-select brokerage and investment management portfolio	18.11%	10 years
• Noble Corporation (oil rigs)	17.36%	10 years

Rates shown are no guarantee of future performance.

Company or Investment	Avg Annual % Return	Number of Years
• Excelsior Value and Restructuring	15%	10 years
• Bridgeway Fund	21%	10 years
• Equity One (REIT)	20%	6 years
• Archer Daniels Midland	28.6%	5 years
• Schlumberger largest oil service company in the world, serves 120 countries	17.7%	5 years
• Bruce Fund (Nasdaq symbol BRUFX)	35%	5 years
• R.S. Global Natural Resources	26.8%	5 years
• CVS Pharmacy	17.5%	5 years
• United Health Group 2000-2005	31.95%	5 years
• Valero Energy Corporation Largest independent oil refining company in the U.S. Produces 20% of gasoline in U.S.	129% 99%	2005 2004
• Dividend Paying Stocks		

Rates shown are no guarantee of future performance.

When one door closes, another opens,
but we often look so long and regretfully upon the closed door,
we do not see the ones which open for us.
ALEXANDER GRAHAM BELL

Purchasing Securities

If you are wondering, "How do I purchase stocks?" There are numerous ways, and here are the most common:

- Directly from the company with no or very little cost. This is called "no load."
- There are a number of companies on the Internet where you can buy and sell stock very cost effectively.
- Look in the yellow pages under stockbrokers.
  ~ Discount brokers, such as Charles Schwab & Co. Inc.
  ~ Full-service brokers, such as Citigroup

How Do I Know What Stocks to Buy?

- Follow the trends. Gas, oil, and commodities are expensive and prices continue to go up, which drives up the stock.
- Another sector, which is very hot and will continue to be, is the alternative fuel-sector. This includes solar, wind, nuclear, bionics, ethanol, etc.
- The most recession-proof industry in the world is utilities. Subscribe to *Utility Forecaster.* It is packed full of helpful information and recommendations. There are many excellent investments in this field. Utilities are a safe haven and are about 4% of the entire investment field.
- Take five minutes daily to review the financial section of your local newspaper.
- There is a wealth of information on the Internet about every publicly owned company.
- Subscribe to *Kiplinger's Personal Finance.* Excellent, inexpensive, and your subscription will be tax deductible.
- Subscribe to the monthly journal called *Smart Money* from *The Wall Street Journal.*

If a business does well, the stock eventually follows.
WARREN BUFFETT

Resources
Books
> *The Intelligent Investor* by Benjamin Graham
>
> *How to Get Started in Stocks* by Paul Larson, Morningstar, Inc.
> *How to Refine Your Stock Strategy* by Paul Larson, Morningstar, Inc.
> *How to Select Winning Stocks* by Paul Larson, Morningstar, Inc.
>
> *Investing for Dummies* by Eric Tyson
>
> *One Up On Wall Street: How To Use What You Already Know*
> *To Make Money In The Market*
> by Peter Lynch and John Rothchild
>
> *Preferreds: Wall Street's Best-Kept Income Secret* by Kenneth G. Winans
> PreferredsTheBook.com
>
> *The Warren Buffett Way, Second Edition* by Robert G. Hagstrom

Discount Stock Broker (largest)
> Charles Schwab & Co. Inc
> > 800-435-4000
> > schwab.com

Factoring/Accounts Receivable
> American Cash Flow Corporation
> > 800-874-0388
> > americancashflow.com/
> > > Provides training on 64 income streams

Stocks
> Pacific West Capital Group
> > 800-588-8000

Investment Results at an Annual Rate of 15%

Invest Each Month	Total $ Invested	Principal & Interest 10 yrs	Total $ Invested	Principal & Interest 15 yrs	Total $ Invested	Principal & Interest 20 yrs	Total $ Invested	Principal & Interest 25 yrs	Total $ Invested	Principal & Interest 30 yrs
$10	$1,200	$2,630	$1,800	$6,164	$2,400	$13,271	$3,000	$27,566	$3,600	$56,318
$15	$1,800	$3,945	$2,700	$9,245	$3,600	$19,906	$4,500	$41,348	$5,400	$84,477
$20	$2,400	$5,260	$3,600	$12,327	$4,800	$26,541	$6,000	$55,131	$7,200	$112,635
$25	$3,000	$6,575	$4,500	$15,409	$6,000	$33,177	$7,500	$68,914	$9,000	$140,794
$50	$6,000	$13,151	$9,000	$30,818	$12,000	$66,354	$15,000	$137,828	$18,000	$281,589
$75	$9,000	$19,726	$13,500	$46,227	$18,000	$99,531	$22,500	$206,742	$27,000	$422,383
$100	$12,000	$26,302	$18,000	$61,637	$24,000	$132,707	$30,000	$275,656	$36,000	$563,177
$200	$24,000	$52,604	$36,000	$123,273	$48,000	$265,415	$60,000	$551,312	$72,000	$1,126,354
$300	$36,000	$78,905	$54,000	$184,910	$72,000	$398,122	$90,000	$826,968	$108,000	$1,689,531
$400	$48,000	$105,207	$72,000	$246,546	$96,000	$530,829	$120,000	$1,102,624	$144,000	$2,252,708
$500	$60,000	$131,509	$90,000	$308,183	$120,000	$663,537	$150,000	$1,378,280	$180,000	$2,815,885
$1,000	$120,000	$263,018	$180,000	$616,366	$240,000	$1,327,073	$300,000	$2,756,561	$360,000	$5,631,770
$2,000	$240,000	$526,036	$360,000	$1,232,731	$480,000	$2,654,147	$600,000	$5,513,122	$720,000	$11,263,541
$3,000	$360,000	$789,055	$540,000	$1,849,097	$720,000	$3,981,220	$900,000	$8,269,682	$1,080,000	$16,895,311

Invest Each Month	Total $ Invested	Principal & Interest 35 yrs	Total $ Invested	Principal & Interest 40 yrs	Total $ Invested	Principal & Interest 45 yrs	Total $ Invested	Principal & Interest 50 yrs
$10	$4,200	$114,148	$4,800	$230,467	$5,400	$464,424	$6,000	$934,997
$15	$6,300	$171,223	$7,200	$345,700	$8,100	$696,636	$9,000	$1,402,495
$20	$8,400	$228,297	$9,600	$460,933	$10,800	$928,849	$12,000	$1,869,993
$25	$10,500	$285,371	$12,000	$575,167	$13,500	$1,161,061	$15,000	$2,337,491
$50	$21,000	$570,742	$24,000	$1,152,334	$27,000	$2,322,121	$30,000	$4,674,983
$75	$31,500	$856,113	$36,000	$1,728,500	$40,500	$3,483,182	$45,000	$7,012,474
$100	$42,000	$1,141,484	$48,000	$2,304,667	$54,000	$4,644,243	$60,000	$9,349,965
$200	$84,000	$2,282,969	$96,000	$4,609,334	$108,000	$9,283,486	$120,000	$18,699,931
$300	$126,000	$3,424,453	$144,000	$6,914,001	$162,000	$13,932,729	$180,000	$28,049,896
$400	$168,000	$4,565,938	$192,000	$9,218,668	$216,000	$18,576,971	$240,000	$37,399,862
$500	$210,000	$5,707,422	$240,000	$11,523,335	$270,000	$23,221,214	$300,000	$46,749,827
$1,000	$420,000	$11,414,844	$480,000	$23,046,671	$540,000	$46,422,428	$600,000	$93,499,654
$2,000	$840,000	$22,829,688	$960,000	$46,093,341	$1,080,000	$92,884,857	$1,200,000	$186,999,309
$3,000	$1,260,000	$34,244,532	$1,440,000	$69,140,012	$1,620,000	$139,327,285	$1,800,000	$280,498,963

The purpose of all examples in this book is to encourage you to begin investing. The calculations are from an interactive online calculator and are not intended to provide investment advice.

Lehman Brother Brokerage
800-582-4904
Ask for department that handles 10 uncommon stocks

Canadian General Investment, Limited (CGI)
866-443-6097

R.S. Global Natural Resources
800-766-3863

Subscriptions (tax deductible)
A Guide to Buying Stocks Without a Broker from Drip Investor
800-233-5922
dripinvestor.com
Kiplinger's Personal Finance
800-544-0155
kiplinger.com
Money
800-633-9970
money.com
The No-Load Fund Investor
800-706-6364
noloadfundinvestor.com
SmartMoney from *The Wall Street Journal*
800-444-4204
smartmoney.com
Utility Forecaster
800-832-2330
utilityforecaster.com

Tax Lien Investor Education/Tax Lien Certificates
877-265-5508
taxlienauthority.com

> *There's nothing like a dream to create the future.*
> VICTOR HUGO

Chapter 13 | *Legally Lower Your Income Taxes*

Tax Freedom Day®

In 2007, Tax Freedom Day, in observance of the number of days Americans work to pay off taxes, will be April 30 (based on 365 working days per year). The rest of the year they will work to support themselves. This includes hundreds of taxes people don't even know about. In fact, every loaf of bread has 72 different taxes hidden in its price. As one IRS auditor stated, "The trick is to stop thinking of it as your money." If you work for 50 years, 16.4 years will be to pay taxes.

IN 2007, AMERICANS WILL WORK	
43 days	Individual Income Taxes
30 days	Social Insurance Taxes
16 days	Sales and Excise Taxes
12 days	Property Taxes
14 days	Corporate Income Taxes
4 days	Other Taxes
1 day	Estate and Gift Taxes
120 days	Total worked for taxes
	Federal (79) State and Local (41)
13 days	Clothing and accessories
30 days	Food
52 days	Health and medical care
62 days	Housing and household operation
22 days	Recreation
30 days	Transportation

A little boy wrote God a letter, asking $100 for Christmas so he could purchase gifts for his family. The postal service sent it to Washington, D.C. because its only address was "God, U.S.A." The politician who received it sent $5 to the boy. Delighted with the $5, the little boy sat down to write a thank-you note to God, which read: "Dear God, Thank you very much for sending the money, however, I noticed that for some reason you had to send it through Washington, D.C. and as usual, those crooks deducted $95."

Many politicians would have us believe that middle- and low-income brackets pay all the taxes while the rich pay none. Though the idea is great for votes, the facts are different:

- The top 10% of taxpayers pay 61% of all income tax.
- The top 22% of taxpayers pay 42% of all income tax.
- The bottom 40% of taxpayers pay less than 1% of all income tax, yet require the bulk of all federal, state, and local expenditures.

Current Tax System

This chapter could include all the reasons the current tax system doesn't work: it's too complicated for anyone to understand, it encourages cheating, it's time-consuming and costly to prepare taxes, taxes are too high, and there are too many of them.

And this would not be new information, so why repeat it here?

Do we need a different and easier tax system? I think everyone reading this book would agree with an emphatic and resounding yes. Yet, until the current tax system is changed, let's talk about some possibilities of how to work with the one we have.

How to Legally Lower Income Taxes with the Current Tax System

Now let's get your taxes reduced so you have more money to invest. This list was accurate when this book was printed. Please consult your CPA or tax attorney as there are frequent tax law changes.

$ For those who qualify, get an interest-only home mortgage loan and have up to $8,000 per year in lower income taxes. See Chapter 9.

$ The greatest tax reduction in IRS history is home sale profits, $250,000 if single and $500,000 if married. If you plan to sell your appreciated home soon, remember these amounts are

100% tax-free and you can repeat the procedure every two years if you have great appreciation and like to move. (See your CPA for circumstances that allow less than two years.)

$ **Pension Plans**

The next most important way to reduce income tax is your pension plans. You notice this is plural. Max out as many of them as allowed.

> For the cash-rich, high-income sole proprietorships and S-company owners who are age 50 and older can stash away as much as $175,000 a year for themselves.
> *The Kiplinger Letter*, April 26, 2006.

Solo 401(k) for self-employed.

> You can invest up to $44,000 for husband and $44,000 for wife for total of $88,000 per year, all tax-free.

401(k) for employees whose employers have 401(k) plan.

> You can deduct from payroll taxes $15,000 or $20,000 if age 50 or older, up to 2009. If company has a matching plan, this equals 100% return year after year.

> "Leaving money in your employer's 401(k) plan can pay off: You can start taking penalty-free withdrawals a little earlier than the normal age of 59 ½. The penalty doesn't apply to payout from company plans after you terminate employment if you are 55 or older in the year you leave. If you roll over the plan balance to an IRA, the penalty applies to withdrawals taken before age 59 ½."
> *Kiplinger Personal Financial Advisor*, November 2006

403(b) for employees of nonprofits such as schools, hospitals, and other tax-exempt 501(c)(3) organizations.

> You can deduct $15,000 per year or $20,000 if you are age 50 and above. This is good to at least 2009.

Simple IRA for employers with 100 or fewer employees.
Employees can contribute $10,000 per year or $12,500 if age 50 or above.

SEP – for sole proprietors, partnerships, corporations, nonprofits, and government entities.
Contribution limit is 25% of pay (20% for self-employed) up to $44,000 per year.

Roth IRA
Income limit is $110,000 for single tax returns and $160,000 for joint tax returns. The annual contribution is $4,000 for each working individual. No tax deduction is allowed. This is best for children who have no tax liability or are at the lower "kiddie tax rate."

Traditional IRA
The annual contribution is $4,000 for each working individual. An additional $1,000 can be contributed if age 50 or older. If you participate in an employer's tax-deductible pension plan, the IRA is not tax-deductible.

412(i) is a simple defined benefit plan. (See Resources)
If you are age 40 or older, and have a small business or profession:

~ Large annual tax deductions (up to $300,000)
~ Plan benefits are fully guaranteed
~ No investment risk, safety of principal
~ Plan contributions are fully tax-deductible
~ Plan assets can grow tax-free
~ Plan assets are protected from judgment creditors
~ Plan is eligible for IRA rollover
~ Lower administration fees
~ Plan is approved **in writing** by IRS
~ Ideal plan for doctors, dentists, small-business owners, and self-employed

It's obvious that whichever category you fit in, pension plans are at the top of the list to reduce your income taxes and immediately invest the money for yourself.

$ Deduct charitable contributions.

$ Self-employed individual.

> When you work out of your home, you have more legal tax deductions than any other trade, skill, or profession. You are able to deduct more costs, thus reducing your income tax and having more money to invest.

$ Maximize IRA and/or Roth IRAs for your children.

> The IRS ruled that you, as a parent, can employ and pay your children once they reach age 7.

$ If you are one of the 80% of taxpayers who received an average $2,500 tax refund this year, go to your Human Resources Department and increase your dependents on a new W-4 form to increase your take-home pay and then invest the extra money **immediately**.

$ Invest in tax-preferred securities and/or tax-exempt bonds.

$ Deduct home property taxes, interest paid on second home.

$ Deduct investment interest, including for home equity line of-credit.

$ Gas and oil partnership.

> Example: $20,000 is typical for one unit. In the first year you can deduct 89%, plus 25% income tax deduction on every monthly check you receive.

$ Have a buy-sell agreement on your business before you sell your business or pass away, to save estate, probate, and other taxes. See a tax attorney.

$ The tax law changes of the past three years have new deductions. See a tax attorney.

$ See Appendix for *2000 Ways to Lower Income Taxes*.

> *It is very possible to become wealthy*
> *without making any more money than you currently make.*
> *Wealth lies in diverting*
> *your hard-earned tax money back to you.*

General Tax Consequences of Four Types of Income

The key to becoming wealthy is the ability to convert earned income (salary and wages) into portfolio, passive, and self-employed income as quickly as possible.

	Work Hard for Your Money	Money Working Hard for You		
	Salary or Wages	Portfolio Income (Securities)	Passive Income (Real Estate)	Self-Employed Income*
Income Assumed	$1,000	$1,000	$1,000	$1,000
Taxable	100%	15%	-0-	-0-
Tax due based on 30% F & S tax bracket	$300	$150	-0-	-0-
Net left after taxes	$700	$850	$1,000	$1,000

*There are no taxes at this point because self-employed working out of their home have more income tax deductions than any other skill, trade, or profession, including almost $100,000 in tax-deductible pension plans alone.

Types of Tax-Free Income
$ **Child Support**
Tax-free to receiver
$ **Alimony**
Can be tax-free if both parties agree
$ **Property Settlement between spouses in a divorce**
Not taxable to the recipient
$ **Company-Borrowed Money**
You can borrow up to $50,000 from your company's pension plan.
$ **Workers' Compensation**

$ **Gain on sale of your home**

You pay no taxes on gains up to $250,000 if single, or $500,000 on a joint tax return. You qualify if you owned and used the home for two out of five years before sale of home, regardless of your age.

$ **Life Insurance**

- Beneficiary receives life insurance proceeds tax-free.
- Life insurance dividends are considered a partial return of premiums you have paid, therefore they are not taxed.

$ **Annuity Payments**

The portion of annuity payments that represents your return of your investment is tax-free.

$ **Pension IRA**

Distributions from non-tax-deductible contributions are not taxed because they were taxed originally.

$ **Rollovers**

No taxes due on any lump sum payout from employer pension plan, provided you reinvest within 90 days in another qualified plan.

$ **Education Saving Bonds**

Most do not have to pay tax on U.S. Series EE and I Saving Bonds issued after December 31, 1989, if the interest is used for educational costs.

$ **Damage Awards**

Awards from a lawsuit for injury or sickness.

$ **Disability Payments**

Accident and health insurance income: If premium was paid by the taxpayer, the benefits are not taxable. If paid by the employer, the benefits are taxable.

$ **Educational Grants**

These are tax-free if you are working on a degree and the money is used strictly for tuition, fees, books, and not for room and board.

$ **Social Security Payments**

If your yearly income is under $25,000 if filing singly or $32,000 for married couples filing jointly, it is tax-free.

$ **Gifts you receive**

$ **Foreign Earned Income**

The first $80,000 per year earned in another country is not taxed to you in the U.S. as long as you were a resident of the foreign country for the tax year. Substantial housing expenses are also tax-free by the U.S.

$ **Inheritance**

It will be tax-free to heirs **only** if pre-death tax planning was done.

$ **State Income Tax Refunds**

Are not taxable if you did not itemize deductions on your federal tax the preceding year.

$ **Employee Awards**

Up to $400 in value

$ **Federal Income Tax Refunds**

$ **Municipal Bond Interest**

Not taxed on your federal return and in many cases not on state and local returns.

$ **Employer Fringe Benefits**

Reimbursed travel and entertainment expenses, pension plans, health and accident insurance, up to $50,000 life insurance, adoption assistance, child and dependent care expenses, employee discounts, transit passes (up to $100/month).

LONG-TERM SOLUTIONS

Some years ago *Money* magazine editors got a group of tax specialists together to develop a typical family's income tax return. The specialists reworked the income tax return until it was correct. Then the editors sent the raw data from the return to the tax preparer specialist in the largest CPA firm in each state. The bottom line? Not one of the 50 companies got the right answer! In fact, the shocking results were from 123% overpayment to 14% underpayment for the one typical family income tax return!

No one (CPAs, attorneys, Congress, IRS agents, not even the IRS commissioner himself) knows the entire U.S. tax code. The current system is broken beyond repair. It is just too complicated.

The long-term solution is:

$ A national retail sales tax to replace current tax systems.

$ Constitutional amendment for a U.S. balanced budget.

$ Restrict government spending increases each year to 60% of annual inflation.

$ Pass a law to eliminate pork-barrel and other nonessential spending and enforce it with the threat of a jail sentence.

$ No new government programs until fraud and waste are brought under control.

$ Reduce free government programs from 20,000 to 500.

$ Pay off the national debt and save more than $5,000 per household per year in interest alone.

Most taxpayers overpay taxes. The sooner that honest taxpayers legally reduce all taxes paid, the sooner Congress will have to abolish the current system and come up with a new plan, such as a national retail sales tax where everyone, from the womb to the tomb, pays.

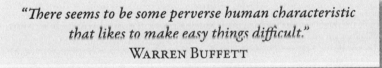

"There seems to be some perverse human characteristic that likes to make easy things difficult."
WARREN BUFFETT

A National Sales Tax

The 17% flat tax being proposed would still encourage tax avoidance by 100 million non-taxpayers. Nothing would change.

The nice thing about the national sales tax is each person decides how much tax he/she will pay by the amount of purchases made. With no deductions whatsoever, everyone would pay a small percentage. The more one spends, the more taxes one pays. It's that simple.

Some will argue the low-income group should be exempt. I disagree, because it has nothing to do with income and everything to do with money spent. Every person pays the tax when something is bought. You buy, you pay! **Every person** would pay his/her fair share.

Examples of Potential Income Tax Reductions and Savings per Year

	Combined Federal and State Income Tax Bracket		
	17%	34%	44%
Interest-only home mortgage $18,000 interest/year (Chapter 9)	$3,060	$6,120	$7,920
401(k) or 403(b) retirement plan, $15,000/year contribution	$2,550	$5,100	$6,600
Home property taxes $2,500/year	$425	$850	$1,100
Investment interest $5,000/year	$850	$1,700	$2,200
Gas and oil partnership 89% deduction the first year $20,000 investment	$3,026	$6,052	$7,832
Charitable contributions $5,000/year	$850	$1,700	$2,200
Home business deductions $10,000/year	$1,700	$3,400	$4,400
Your annual income tax is lowered by this amount by doing the above	$12,461	$24,922	$32,252

This is money you get to keep and invest for yourself!

> *A person doesn't know how much he has to be thankful for until he has to pay taxes on it.*
> AUTHOR UNKNOWN

Advantages of a National Sales Tax

More Americans are demanding tax reform. The need for change is acute. The results would be:

$ Pay less than half of the proposed flat tax
$ It's exceedingly simple, retailers already collect state sales tax
$ Tax would be collected once
$ Simplified tax code—You buy, you pay
$ No deductions—period
$ An immediate and powerful impact on the level of economic activity
$ A radical shift from consumption to investing
$ Allows individuals to earn as much as they choose so they have more to invest for themselves and the nation
$ America's international competitiveness would increase
$ Increased jobs and standard of living in U.S.
$ Increased savings and investments in U.S.
$ Improved civil liberties
$ All citizens treated the same, extreme fairness
$ 100% of Americans pay
$ Maintain your privacy
$ Enjoy April 15
$ Tax advice not needed or paid for
$ Reduced lobbying
$ No more IRS, filing income taxes and deadlines, loopholes in exchange for political support, tax audits, income tax, corporate tax, death tax, inheritance tax, capital gains tax, gift tax, payroll tax, withholding tax

Actions You Can Take Now

$ Write, call, or email your Congressional representatives.
$ Work with groups that promote the national sales tax.
$ Share this information with family, friends, and co-workers. Have them write their Congressional representative as well.
$ Write letters to the members of the president's committees who are studying the tax system and looking for ways to improve it.

Resources

Bob Carlson's *Retirement Watch*

For help with the following:

~ A tax break with steady income

~ Tax shelters for corporate owners

~ Which investments for tax-deferred accounts

~ Deducting your investments as a business

~ Big tax breaks for no cash

800-552-1152

retirementwatch.com

Book

422 Tax Deductions: For Businesses and Self-Employed Individuals
by Bernard B. Kamoroff, CPA

If you pay excessive income tax

412(i) information

Guardian Life Insurance Company of America

Chris Hunken

2550 Compass Road, Suite H

Glenview, Illinois 60026

847-564-0123

Koresko & Associates

John Koresko, Tax Attorney and CPA

200 W. 4th Street

Bridgeport, Pennsylvania 19405

610-992-2200

Web site

taxfoundation.org

*I'm proud to pay taxes in the United States;
the only thing is, I could be just as proud for half the money.*
ARTHUR GODFREY

Chapter 14 | *Invest in Energy with Little of Your Own Energy*

Oil as an Investment

There is probably no safer investment than energy and no doubt the safest energy investments are in the United States and Canada. Global demand is expected to triple by mid-century.

There are dozens of ways to invest in oil. A few are:

$ Manufacturers of oil well platforms
$ Manufacturers of components for the entire oil industry
$ Service companies to the oil industry
$ Companies that explore for oil (some are called wildcatters)
$ Established oil drilling companies
$ Tanker ships
$ Transportation systems to refineries
$ Pipeline companies
$ Refineries
$ Companies that transport to gas stations
$ Gas stations

Remember, even in a great investment category such as gas and oil you need to diversify. Subscribe to one or more of the newsletters for up-to-date information. The following are a few examples of companies that have done well in the past:

Companies listed are for information purposes only.
Past performance is no guarantee of future results.
The information has been gathered from excellent sources, and
the author cannot guarantee the accuracy of the information.

- **ARC Energy** (AET.UN)
- **Chevron**
  The second-largest oil company in the U.S. (NYSE:CVX)
- **Enerplus Resources**
  The largest natural gas and oil company in Canada. In 2005 the appreciation and dividends was 44%. For the past ten years, they have been 32.9%. The annual 9%-12% dividend is paid monthly. They keep out 15% tax, which is not duplicated in the United States so you pay it only once. As an American you cannot let the dividends stay in to be reinvested. (NYSE:ERF)
- **Exxon Mobil**
  The world's largest oil and gas company. They do everything from exploration to owning gas stations. (NYSE:XOM)
- **Valero Energy Corporation**
  They are the number-one refiner in North America, with headquarters in San Antonio, Texas. Ranked number three on Fortune's 2006 list of top 100 best companies to work for. They were ranked third-best-performing stock out of 11,000 by Forbes in 2005. They had a 180% five-year total cumulative shareholder return. (NYSE:VLO)
- **Nal Oil and Gas** (NAE.UN)
- **Noble Corporation**
  An 82-year-old company that builds and leases gigantic deep-water oil drilling rigs. Currently they have 63 leased to companies in 13 countries. Their stock has averaged 46.9% appreciation per year for the past 20 years. (NYSE:NE)
- **Schlumberger**
  The largest oil service company in the world. It services 120 countries. From undertaking three-dimensional seismic analyses of oil and gas deposits to bringing in complete wells, Schlumberger's technologies expertise is unmatched. So far this year their stock is up 25%, and 45% more than last year. For the past five years their stock increased 17.7% per year and 15% the past 10 years. With crude oil prices staying in the $50 to $100

range, this stock should do great. (NYSE:SLB)
- **Vermilion Energy** (VET.UN-T)

Canada had the second-highest stock market growth in the world in 2005. Some examples for your consideration:

Canadian Resource Stock Returns		
COMPANY	STOCK SYMBOL	2005 RETURN
Petro-Canada	(PC2)	58%
Glamis Gold	GLG	60%
Encana	ECC	61%
Faloonbridge	Fal	71%
Suncor	SU	79%
Cameo	CCJ	82%
Talisman Energy	TLM	97%
CDN Natural Resources	CNQ	133%

There are several energy companies listed above, and all are diversified in different areas of the industry. The best way to learn about oil, gas, and utility stocks would be to subscribe to a top long-term newsletter (see Resources).

The Demand for Oil

The reason usually given for high gas prices is supply and demand. This is correct. And the reasons go much deeper and include:

- World population is quickly headed toward 8 billion and demand for energy increases.
- Crude oil consumption has increased annually for the past 23 years in the United States alone.
- For each two barrels of oil the world consumes per year, only one is replaced from new and smaller oil discoveries.

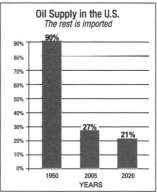

- United States supply of oil and gas is rapidly being used up nor does it have sufficient refining capacity.
- Environmental issues
- More than 12 countries that were oil exporters now have become importers of oil.
- Saudi Arabia and Iran now consume 35% of their oil production compared to only 5% a few years ago.
- Developing countries such as India and China are searching the world to secure energy supplies for their growing economies. Many major cities in China face daily electrical shortages of up to 50% due to their rapid growth of almost 10% per year for the past 20 years. Their energy demand has not kept up with growth. Auto sales have increased at the rate of 20% per year with many of its almost 1.4 billion citizens reaching middle class. China's current, intermediate, and long-range energy needs are awesome.

China has quietly and rapidly searched the world over for energy supplies. They have invested billions in Venezuela, Argentina, Brazil, Bolivia, Ecuador, Canada, and Colombia. In a few short years, China went from an oil exporter to importing 7 million barrels a day, which will double in the next 10 years.

Natural Gas—Skyrocketing Demand
- **Commercial Use**
  Office buildings, hospitals, schools, churches, hotels, and restaurants use it for cooling, space and water heating.
- **Economic and Population Growth**
  The U.S. population is more than 300 million, and by 2015 it will be 330 million.
- **Electricity Generation**
  Strict emission control has mandated clean-burning natural gas and has increased usage. Almost 100% of all new operation plants being built will consume natural gas.

- **Fuel Cells**

  Many fuel cells use natural gas to generate electric power.
- **Industrial Use**

  Natural gas is a base ingredient for plastic, fertilizer, anti-freeze, fabric, etc. Industry uses 43% of all natural gas.
- **Residential Use**

  Natural gas is used in 70% of new homes for heat in the winter and air conditioning in the summer.
- **Transportation Sector**

  Today 110,000 vehicles burn natural gas and the number increases daily.

Natural Gas and Liquid Natural Gas

Many of the investments in the oil sector also apply to natural gas because many of the companies are involved in both gas and oil.

Because of the tremendous shortage of natural gas in the United States, other countries with extra supply have developed a new industry to convert natural gas to liquid natural gas (LNG).

LNG is transported inexpensively to the United States in highly specialized ships with special reinforced tanks under very low temperature. Once these tankers arrive here, the liquid is converted back to a gas and piped to various destinations throughout the country. Currently there are several LNG terminals in use, several more under construction, and more than 30 new building sites have been proposed in the US.

This is America's salvation, along with natural gas imports from Canada, our dear neighbors to the north.

Renewable and Alternative Energy Is Needed NOW!

America learned nothing from the 1973 oil embargo. At that point America should have laid out a master plan to be energy self-sustained by the year 2000. Instead, America owns less than 3% of the world's oil reserves, and accounts for more than 25% of the daily oil consumption (almost 21 million barrels). **The world consumes a billion barrels of oil every 11.76 days.** The output from established wells continues to decline, and, when a well runs dry—it is done. (You know the funny sound you hear when the soda is gone and you start sucking up air? It is the same with oil.) In addition, the U.S. consumes 61 billion cubic feet of natural gas daily.

As we release ourselves from foreign energy imports, the standard of living in the U.S. will improve and our standing as a world power will grow.

The United States has a small alternative fuel program that needs to be larger and more comprehensive. We need to do like Brazil, which set up a master plan for alternative fuel. There 90% of all cars and trucks burn ethanol exclusively and shortly it will be 100%. Brazil is the first country to accomplish such a worthwhile achievement.

Possible alternative fuel choices to invest in are: biodiesel (from soybeans), biofuels, bran, electricity, ethonol (from corn), geothermal, grass, hydride batteries, hydrogen cells, natural gas, ocean power, rapeseed, solar, sugarcane, wind, water, nuclear, and uranium. One company, Archer Daniels Midland, has had 28.6% return in the past five years.

Resources
Enerplus Resources
    800-319-6462

Solar Living Institute
    707-744-2017   solarliving.org/

Subscriptions (tax-deductible)
    Roger Conrad's *Utility Forecaster* (this is excellent)
        800-832-2330   utilityforecaster.com
    Outstanding Investments
        800-326-1433   agorafinancial.com
    Czeschin's Oil & Energy Investment Report
        843-388-2668
    The Complete Investor
        866-833-2070   completeinvestor.com/

If America, as we know it, is going to be saved, a gigantic, rapid surge of combined effort needs to happen now to make renewable and alternative energy a reality.

Chapter 15 | *How to Really Make It in Real Estate*

> *"More money has been made in real estate than in all industrial investments combined."*
> ANDREW CARNEGIE

Quite a statement—and how true it is: *More millionaires have been made from real estate than any other investment.*

Almost all wealthy people have various types of investments in their portfolio; and more than 98% always have real estate and securities. The beginning investor and young people should take this very seriously. Want to be wealthy? Do what wealthy people do—invest in real estate!

In addition, parents should teach their children to purchase real estate even if they start out with only $500 a year. One family gives an income property to each child on his or her birthday. What an awesome way to create wealth at an early age!

The secret to purchasing real estate, regardless if it is your home, investment properties, etc., is never to use your own money. Use borrowed money, which is called "leverage." You should pay interest only on money for investments, which is okay because you are using the borrowed money to make more money.

If you have purchased income-producing real estate, the interest and all expenses are tax deductible. Even on your own home, the interest and property taxes are tax deductible. Consequently, each month you have more cash in your hand because you are not sending it to Washington. Now every month you have more cash to invest for yourself.

I remember graduating with my master's degree from Florida State University and moving to Southern California for my first job. Even though my wife and I were debt-free, including a brand-new car, we had no money to purchase a home. And we chose to live on my salary and invest 100% of my wife's.

In six months, we purchased a beautiful large lot in an orange grove and hired an architect to design our dream ranch-style home. When the design was complete, the house was too large for the lot (because of the required set-back law). I immediately purchased the lot next door, took 25 feet from it, put the rest of the lot back on the market, and sold it in two weeks for the same price I paid for the original lot. These two lots were my first experience in making money in real estate.

We rented for only one year then moved into our lovely new home built with 95% borrowed money. Every property I purchased since then was with 100% other people's money.

Renting

Renting for life will keep you from achieving your financial goals while you make other people millionaires.

Have you stopped to figure how much money you waste renting? Assume you start renting at age 25 and live to 85. That's 60 years. Let's assume the average rent paid was $1,000 per month. That's $12,000 a year. In 60 years you would spend $720,000. All you have to show for it is a stack of worthless rent receipts, 720 of them.

Home Ownership Can Make You a Multimillionaire

Purchase your own home as soon as possible. See Chapter 9. You could be averaging $252,152 per year for life just from home ownership. Naturally, this figure will vary depending on your federal and state income tax bracket and your mortgage rate. Even if your returns were $50,000 to $100,000 per year for life, that would be an awesome supplement to your other income.

Three years to the week that we moved into our first home, I was promoted to another job in Southern California. We sold our lovely home and made a great profit. With our profit we purchased two properties at our new location. One lot had a large home, which we lived in, and a small rental unit in the back. The second property had two homes on a very large lot.

Now we had three renters with a positive cash flow. This, my dear friend, was the last time I ever put my own money down to purchase any property.

A year later we purchased and moved to a large, exquisite home on top of a hill overlooking a manicured golf course; we also had a view of five mountain ranges. Again I purchased that home with none of my own money.

My next venture into real estate was in northern Vermont where my wife grew up. We would visit there once or twice a year and I quickly fell in love with the area. Two of my brothers-in-law owned dairy farms and soon I purchased, with a $500 check, my first dairy farm. The money came from my home equity line-of-credit so again I purchased property with zero of my money. The farm was rented out and there were excellent tax deductions. My properties made it possible for me to pay zero income taxes for years.

Between the ages of 40-45, I gave $11 million to my favorite charities, a mistake I have regretted many times over. If I had compounded the $11 million, today I could write a check for $11 million to each of 273 different charities. Most of the money came from real estate profit and other investments. This is my 50th year of earning an average of 15% on all my investments. You, too, can do the same!

Advantages of Owning Your Own Home

$ **Privacy**
When you own and live in your own home, you have gigantically more privacy, peace, and quiet than when crammed into an apartment complex.

$ **Way to Wealth**
Real estate is the average family's way to wealth.

$ **Inflation**
You are able to keep ahead of inflation in most areas of the country.

$ **Appreciation**
The U. S. Labor Department stated the average home in America doubles in value every 26 years. In many parts of the country it is far less time. My home, in California, has doubled in value more than nine times in the past 26 years. So it all depends on where you live.

$ **Source of Funds for Investing**

Use your home equity, whether your home is paid for or not. See Chapter 9.

$ **Home Equity Line-of-Credit**

This is the best banking concept, in my opinion. It is the greatest thing since baseball, motherhood, and apple pie. Once you get approved, you have a special personal checkbook to write your own loans whenever you want, for whatever reason you want, without checking with anyone. I use mine for investments and pay only the interest each month. The rates are reasonable.

$ **Deductibility**

You can deduct your interest from your home equity line-of-credit, your regular mortgage interest, and property taxes.

$ **Limited Risk**

Your home investment is one of the most risk-free investments available.

$ **Tax-Free Cash**

The greatest gift ever voted by Congress was the law that allows us to sell our appreciated home and pay zero taxes on the appreciation up to $250,000 for a single person and up to $500,000 for married couples provided you have lived in the home two of the past five years. And if you live in a fast-appreciating area, you can repeat the process every two years. That is fantastic!

$ **Peace of Mind**

Saving for Your First Home

If you know you are going to stay put for at least three to five years, I would do everything in your power to purchase your own home immediately. You say, "I do not have the money for a down payment." No problem. You can now get 100% financing for your **first home**. The government and mortgage companies have a number of programs that enable you to purchase your first home without any cash.

If you prefer to have cash saved to put down on your first home purchase, then you may want to incorporate the following ideas as quickly as possible.

- Quickly become debt-free. See Chapter 8.
- Remember the difference between needs and wants. Buy just your needs and apply the rest toward your home purchase.
- Lower your expenses and apply the savings toward your down payment. See Appendix for *2000 Ways to Lower Living Expenses.*
- Lower your income tax so that you have more money to invest for your first home. See Chapter 13. Also see Appendix for *2000 Ways to Lower Income Taxes.*
- Cash value from life insurance.
- Parents or grandparents who can give you a cash gift or low-interest loan.
- If you borrow from a close friend at a reasonable rate of interest, make sure you have a written agreement or note.
- Take a look at your retirement funds for a possible penalty-free, temporary loan.
- Consider selling stocks and other liquid investments such as CDs, etc.
- Consider selling a seldom-used boat, R.V., and other rapidly depreciating unused items.
- Apply all bonuses, income tax refunds, and income from any other sources toward your down payment. The yields will be far greater in your home.

> *Owning a home is a keystone of wealth...*
> *both financial affluence and emotional security.*
> SUZE ORMAN

Supplement Your Income as A Real Estate Investor

Hardly a week goes by that I do not see a display ad in my local newspaper inviting attendees to a free real estate seminar. All of the programs promote the purchase of real estate with zero down, and then selling the property at a nice profit. The free seminars are generally a sales pitch to a paid one-to-three-day training seminar. The cost can run between $350 to several thousand dollars. If you think you would like buying and selling real estate, it is an awesome way to earn an extra $50,000 to $150,000 per year. Remember, you do not need to become a licensed real estate sales person or broker—you are an investor, not a realtor. Good buys on property are always available in good or bad markets. There is at least one home priced below value in every square mile of populated areas.

Here's why people sell real estate below market value.

- Bankruptcy
- Divorce
- Foreclosure
- Health problems
- Inheritance sale
- Loss of job
- Poor management and ignorance
- Relocation
- Retirement
- Tax problems
- Want out now

Real Estate Investment Trusts (REITs)

REITs were created in 1960 as an investment vehicle by Congress. REITs give you the opportunity to own shares of commercial real estate and participate in its growth. Their stock can go up or down just like any other stock. The majority of REITs pay a nice consistent dividend. REIT investments build on growing dividends and give you diversification in your investment portfolio.

REITs own all types of commercial properties: shopping malls, apartment complexes, hospitals, nursing homes, senior housing, etc. There are several types of REITs. The two I like the best are:

- REITs that borrow the money to purchase the properties.
- REITs that finance their own mortgages, thus making added money from the interest, as a bank does. These have a higher rate of return.

Real Estate Portfolio ranks the REITs by profitability and dividends over time. You will find a number that yield 15%-30% ongoing, which will make you very happy. **Free** subscription information is listed in the Resources at the end of the chapter.

Other Sources of Real Estate Income

$ **Real Estate Mutual Funds**
   Check the MorningStar Rating to find the best performers over the long term.

$ **Purchase first or second trust deeds**
   I have done this for years with excellent results. Expect 15%-28% return and have ample equity to protect yourself. If you are new to this type of investment, buy a book on investing in trust deeds. To find trust deeds, look in the yellow pages under "Trust Deed Investment" and check the business or finance classified section of your local newspaper. Another option is to put an ad in the paper "Money to loan for first and second trust deeds," and include your telephone number.

$ **Purchase trust deeds at a discount**
   Your yield will be 20%-30%. For example, you offer $15,000 for a good $20,000 trust deed. In addition to the $5,000, you also get the interest on the monthly payments on the full $20,000 trust deed until it is paid off.

In summary, real estate is stable, proven, reliable, and is in the portfolio of 98% of all wealthy investors. Join the wealthy!

Learn About Real Estate

$ Real Estate Seminar
   The seminar and follow-up I like best is conducted by Carleton Sheets. The main reasons are: he has decades of successful experience as a real estate investor, you don't tie up a weekend because you take the course at

your home at your speed, and the cost is very low. You will learn more than 15 ways to buy property with no down payment, why you don't need good credit to buy property, how to identify good investments, plus additional outstanding information. See Resources.

$ Real Estate Reports - Free

Learn the best way to buy and sell a residence with the most down-to-earth and rewarding methods available today. Bud Minton has been in the real estate business for more than 30 years and has owned four real estate offices. He has advised his clients to make the best use of their assets when selling and buying homes. He now shares his years of experience to help people negotiate the very complex real estate issues. Access the eight extraordinary reports listed in the Resource section.

> *If you want to go somewhere,*
> *it is best to find someone who has already been there.*
> ROBERT KIYOSAKI

Resources
Books
Real Estate Loopholes: Secrets of Successful Real Estate Investing
by Diane Kennedy, Robert T. Kiyosaki, and Garrett Sutton,

Real Estate Riches: How to Become Rich Using Your Banker's Money
by Dolf de Roos and Diane Kennedy

Rich Dad's Advisors®: The ABC's of Real Estate Investing:
The Secrets of Finding Hidden Profits Most Investors Miss
by Ken McElroy

What No One Ever Tells You About Investing in Real Estate:
Real-Life Advice from 101 Successful Investors
by Robert J. Hill and Robert Shemin

Why We Want You to be Rich: Two Men-One Message
    by Donald J. Trump, Robert T. Kiyosaki, Meredith McIver,
    and Sharon Lechter

MorningStar USA
    225 North Michigan Avenue, Suite 700, Chicago, IL 60601
    312-616-1620 or 312-384-4000
    morningstar.com

National Association of Real Estate Investment Trusts
    1875 I Street, NW, Suite 600, Washington, DC 20006-5413
    800-362-7348 or 202-739-9400
    Frequently Asked Questions about REITs
        nareit.com/newsroom/ftseQandA.pdf
    Real Estate Portfolio
        nareit.com/portfoliomag/default.shtml

Real Estate–Buying and Selling
    Bud Minton
    877-203-2008
    budminton.mobi

Real Estate Reports–**Free**
    877-625-4408

#	Topic
5000	Costly Homeseller Mistakes
5004	6 Buyers Mistakes
5014	Save Thousands
5017	For Sale By Owner
5023	27 Valuable Tips to Selling
5025	Zero Down Program
5042	Distress Sale
5048	Fixer Upper

Real Estate Seminar–study at home (very cost effective)
  No Down Payment® Real Estate Program with Carleton H. Sheets
    The Professional Education Institute
      Box 5045, Oak Brook, Illinois 60522-5045
    800-569-1203 or 800-353-5219
    CarletonSheets.com

It's tangible, it's solid, it's beautiful.
It's artistic, from my standpoint,
and I just love real estate.
DONALD TRUMP

| Chapter 16 | *Save Taxes and Protect Your Assets* |

I had an acquaintance with an estate valued at $2 million. The surviving son and daughter expected to each receive $1 million. And, because there was **no estate plan**—the IRS, other taxing entities, and the attorneys took everything. What did the children eventually get?

Nothing!

You may say to yourself, "I don't have much money or assets so I don't need an estate plan." I cannot emphasize enough the need for a **simple estate plan** that will protect your assets so that no more taxes will be paid at your death. You pay taxes all your life (in fact, you will spend more than 16 years of your working life to pay taxes). Why pay them at death as well?

With a simple estate plan, your heirs will be able to celebrate your life instead of meeting with the IRS. You cannot plan your estate if you have Alzheimer's, are on your deathbed, or have passed away. Remember, you want to leave a living legacy for your heirs and favorite charities; what you don't want to leave them is a living hell.

"At the finish line (your death) how do you want the resources that you have accumulated during your lifetime to be used, and whom do you want to benefit? How do you wish to be remembered, and what do you want your legacy to be? The choices available to you now, the decisions you make now and the actions you take will determine the answers to these questions," says Maynard Lowry, Ph.D.

> *There is no need to pay a huge death tax when you die.*
> *Instead, create a simple estate plan and*
> *give the money to your heirs and favorite charity.*

As far as the IRS is concerned, your estate boils down to one word, and that is money. The IRS does not care what you own. They see your estate as a giant funnel with a large faucet at the bottom. All personal property, real estate, life insurance, business interests, automobiles, jewelry, etc. is "dumped" into the funnel. As it goes in, the IRS has everything appraised to a dollar figure and out of the faucet come the dollars.

Where do the dollars go? It's very simple. To pay the IRS death taxes, accounting fees, appraiser's fees, probate fees, attorney's fees, executor's fees, etc. And if there's anything left, the state determines who receives it.

There are three unchangeable facts regarding your estate: You own stuff, you will die, someone will get that stuff. The secret is to leave a perpetual legacy.

$ AN ESTATE IS ONE WORD $
MONEY

Why You Need an Estate Plan—Protect Your Assets

If you apply what you learn from this book, you will be a multimillionaire while you are young enough to enjoy it. With an estate plan you will save taxes and be able to distribute your wealth so that your legacy can live on. Yours will be remembered as a life of inspiration.

$ Keep your estate private at your death.

$ Save your survivors untold grief, trouble, and problems by avoiding probate court. Remember probate is in all 50 states.

     ~ save time, probate can take one to ten years

     ~ save money, probate costs can take up to 25%

       Is this how you want to be remembered?

$ When you earn money, spend money, save money, and die—you are taxed. Even your heirs pay an inheritance tax on the money you leave, that is unless you protect them. Death taxes are an insult and are 100% avoidable.

$ Prevents double or triple taxation.

$ So your heirs won't have to visit the mortuary and the IRS the same week you die.

$ Avoid possible forced liquidation of your estate with financial loss and hardship on family. Just nine months after your death, the IRS expects all taxes due.

$ So that you can provide for the orderly continuance or sale of your business with a buy and sell agreement. Some 63% of all business owners have not made any provision for the transfer of their business, thus paying billions of dollars in unnecessary taxes.

$ This is your last chance to do something great and special for your favorite institution or charity. If you do not act, the IRS could get most of your estate.

The Most Important Legal Documents for Complete Asset Protection

To save maximum taxes and protect your assets completely, you need these basic instruments.	
Will	A legal declaration of how a person wishes his or her possessions to be disposed of after death Includes who takes care of any underage children
Living Trust	Avoids probate court Host of other advantages
Family Limited Partnership	Used since 1916 Protects all assets from lawsuits, if properly written
C-Corporation	Business legal structure Lowers taxes substantially Host of other advantages
Charitable Remainder Trust	Cuts capital gain tax to zero Reduces or eliminates all taxes, including death tax Pays you and your wife for life Pass on your estate to your heirs tax-free
NOTE: To protect yourself and receive all the advantages you must have the exact verbiage in these legal documents. Use the specialist who invented legal asset protection (see Resources).	

> *A estate plan is where you decide
> when and how to give your money away!*

Your Will—The Foundation of Your Simple Estate Plan

What is a will? A will is your legal statement of your wishes concerning the disposal of your property (estate/money) after death. It is the first and most important document of your simple estate plan. It should be prepared by an attorney who specializes in wills and living trusts.

The shocking fact is 80% of all Americans do not even have a will. And according to *USA Today,* "Fifty-three percent of all affluent Americans do not have an estate plan in place." Perhaps they think everything they own automatically goes to their heirs. Wrong, wrong, wrong.

If you do not have a will, please create one now! It is the foundation to everything else you do and the cost is reasonable. Remember that, without a will, the judge will decide who raises your children, and the state will decide who gets your estate/money. Please stop reading right now and call for an appointment with an estate planning attorney to prepare a will and, if needed, a living trust. And do it before you go to bed tonight.

Create a Will and Trust Now...
So you decide who raises your children, not the judge
So you decide who gets your wealth, not the state
So you decide who administers your estate, not the court

Why People Put Off Preparing a Will
- They do not have the will to make out a will.
- Procrastination
    They kid themselves thinking there is plenty of time.
    Seven of my friends passed away in a three-week period.
    Three, under the age of 50, were gone within five minutes from heart attacks.
- It takes time.
    Yes, two days now—or one or two **years** after you die.

- **It is inconvenient to find a good attorney.**
  If you don't have an attorney, call the trust officer at your favorite charity for recommendations.
- **You feel uneasy thinking about your own death.**
  Perhaps you think you might die sooner with a will and an estate plan. This is nonsense.
  You are going to live until you die, period.

> *People who do proper estate planning actually live longer because stress, tension, and pressure are gone.*
> *You will feel great to leave a legacy.*

- **Estate planning is too complicated.**
  Nonsense. It boils down to five words—"**Money, and who gets it**." Your heirs, charity, government, or a combination?
- **It is not important.**
  Rich or poor, you need a will and most of us need a living trust and additional estate planning.
- **There is no need.**
  Perhaps you think everything will go automatically and equally go to all family members. Wrong. Remember: Without a will and living trust, the judge will decide who raises your children, the state will decide who gets your wealth, and probate court will decide who administers your estate.

The Money Can Go Only To...
Your Family
Your Favorite Charity
The Government
OR a Combination of All Three

When you die, do you want to leave a living hell for your heirs, or a living legacy? Only you can make this decision. "I will instruct and guide you and advise you and watch your progress. Do not be like the senseless mule." Psalms 32:8, 9. Are you being a mule about delaying your estate planning?

Prudent people plan now to preserve and distribute their assets as good asset managers. You cannot do this when you are on your deathbed.

Living Trust—Your Second Legal Document

A living trust, an asset management arrangement, is a legal document prepared by an estate planning attorney. Your trust would be called The YourName Family Trust, YourName, Trustee. You transfer all of your large assets (your home, property, stocks, etc.) into the trust. This is imperative or your living trust is worthless. Small items such as computers, household furnishing would be in categories in your will, sometimes referred to as a pour-over will.

You would be the trustee of your living trust while you are alive. The trust gives instruction for managing the trust while you are alive and, then, after your death. See your attorney today.

Advantages of a Living Trust

$ Allows your assets to be transferred immediately to your beneficiaries at no cost by avoiding probate court.

$ Eliminates the time your estate could be tied up in probate court, one to two years is normal. I had a friend with several businesses who passed away without a will and living trust. His case was in probate for 10 years. Can you imagine the living hell his family went through because he did not take two days to develop an estate plan?

$ The cost of probate can run up to 25% of the estate value, robbing the family unnecessarily.

$ Reduces estate taxes.

$ Provides income for surviving spouse, other heirs, and charities.

$ Leaves a living legacy.

$ Provides and ensures privacy.

$ Less likely to create problems between heirs at your death.

$ You can include property from other states in your living trust.

The living trust is the best legal way used by most attorneys to avoid probate court. All 50 states require probate court if a person dies without a will and living trust. The only variation is what triggers the requirement in your state.

For example, in my state of California, if you have an estate over $100,000, you automatically are forced into probate court, that is, if you do not have a living trust. In Washington state, it's only $60,000 of assets that triggers probate. To learn your state's requirements, call the probate division at your local courthouse. Ask them what level of assets requires probate court. If you exceed the requirement, then—by all means—get a living trust immediately. Take two days to save your estate and your heirs untold grief.

Family Limited Partnership

Functions like other limited partnerships, and is composed of family members rather than third-party partners or investors. This has been in use since 1916 and is the only document that protects your assets. It **must** contain the proper wording.

C-Corporation

A C-Corporation is a common business word to distinguish a coporation whose profits are taxed separately from its owners under a subchapter of the IRS code.

Charitable Remainder Trust

The charitable remainder trust is a legal document that has been used as far back as ancient Rome. In modern form, it has been used by many individuals as a means to make gifts while meeting other important objectives, including, but not limited to, protecting your wealth at your death.

> *"At the end of your life, what you will most regret will be the deeds left undone and the words left unspoken."*
> ROBIN SHARMA

Save Money on These Five Important Legal Documents

These five very important documents, when properly written, will:

- $ Protect all your assets
- $ Avoid death or estate taxes
- $ Eliminate capital gains tax
- $ Lower your income tax
- $ Keeps you out of probate court
- $ Save potentially large sums of money

To have these legal documents prepared by an asset protection attorney could cost you $10,000 to $25,000.

The "father of asset protection" is attorney Robert Bluhm. He and his law firm started asset protection 40 years ago and are unquestionably the #1 asset protection firm in the country.

They have created an Asset Protection Kit that contains the five documents with the exact wording necessary to give you **full asset protection**. The kit is simple to use; just fill in the blanks and follow the very simple instructions. I was able to negotiate a special price of $2,995 for readers of this book. ($10,000-$25,000 if you were to use an asset protection attorney). See Resources for order information.

> ### Plan Your Estate…
> Accumulate money
> Conserve your money
> Compound your money
> Distribute your money—when, to whom, how

Plan Your Estate to Save Taxes

The best estate plan leaves the most money to your heirs and favorite charities.

Please do not be part of the Triple 90 Rule: 90% of the time, 90-year-olds have 90% of their estate intact with no plan for distribution. Rather than leave their estate to their favorite charities and heirs, they pay billions of dollars of unnecessary income taxes.

Let me quickly emphasize it is not just 90-year-olds making this mistake. Remember, 80% of all Americans do not even have a simple will, much less a living trust. As a result there are many heartaches and billions lost.

Your goal of your estate plan is to reduce the tax liability and give as much money as possible to heirs and/or charities.

Retirement plans, when left in your estate as deferred income, are taxable at your death. There are up to eight types of taxation on retirement plans that can eat up about 80% of the money. Taxes are charged on your qualified retirement plan assets even if a spouse or other heirs are named beneficiaries.

One gigantically important exception is to give the tax-deferred retirement plan assets to your favorite 501(c)(3) charity. The good news is you do not pay a of penny tax and neither to they.

As you create your estate plan, consider this: Your heirs will receive only about 20 cents on the dollar on the retirement accounts. If you give your retirement plans to your favorite charities, they will receive 100%. Then give your other assets to your heirs and, if planned correctly, they could receive 100 cents on every dollar. Your estate planning attorney or development officer of your favorite charity can be of extreme help to you.

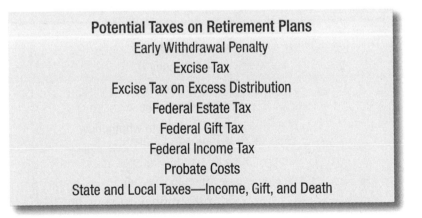

Potential Taxes on Retirement Plans
Early Withdrawal Penalty
Excise Tax
Excise Tax on Excess Distribution
Federal Estate Tax
Federal Gift Tax
Federal Income Tax
Probate Costs
State and Local Taxes—Income, Gift, and Death

Your Final Tax Return—After You Die

I can imagine you are asking, "How can a dead person file an income tax return?" That, my dear friend, is a logical question. The IRS requires the surviving spouse, trustee, or heirs to file a final tax return on behalf of the deceased. If the final tax return is audited, it can be a breeze (if there is an estate plan) or it can be a nightmare (if there is not). And, with an estate plan, the heirs will receive more of the money instead of paying unnecessary taxes.

Did You Make That Call?

Please make an appointment today with the development officer of your favorite charity or with a good estate planning attorney. Have your will, living trust, family limited partnership, C-Corporation, and Charitable Remainder Trust created so your great legacy can live on and on.

Much success to you.

Resources
Asset Protection Kit
 Robert Bluhm, J.D.
 Darin Delaney
 800-968-5450 x 1513
 Negotiated price is $2,995 for readers of this book
  ($10,000-$25,000 if you were to use an asset protection attorney)

Give to Your Favorite Charity...
You give to your favorite charity
and still leave everything to your heirs!
AND YOU
Avoid probate
Avoid the death tax
Avoid capital gains tax
Lower your current income tax
Maintain or increase your income for life

| Chapter 17 | *Prepare for*
 Your Wealthy Retirement |

Retirement

The act of having concluded
one's working or professional career
with the knowledge that the best years are yet to come,
especially if you retire young and wealthy!
PAUL S. DAMAZO

This is based on my opinion that you retire wealthy while young. Retirement is not sitting in a rocking chair waiting to die, it's living the life you came here to live, with the money to pay for it.

Retirement Possibilities

- Second career at your pace
- Go back to school
- Volunteer and give something back
- Hobbies, expand current ones, find new ones
- Travel
- Leisure
- More rest
- Read
- Part-time work

In addition, there are hundreds of organizations that would be happy to use your talents as a volunteer. Many of these involve traveling to almost any part of the world.

A Wealthy Retirement Starts at Birth

As a parent or grandparent, you can start a baby's growth estate for your children and grandchildren as they are born. What do I mean?

Let's face it. Family, relatives, and close friends make up most of the attendees at a baby shower. In the announcement, tell them it's a baby "growth estate shower" and if they would please bring $25 instead of a gift. If 20 guests bring $25 each, that's $500. And you know what? Most will bring the $25—plus a gift!

When the *baby* is ready to retire at age 45, your thoughtful planning will provide $1,616,307 for your son or daughter for their financial freedom. What a great thing to do for your next child! This is the absolute best way I know to prepare for retirement.

Baby's Growth Estate

See what a great financial foundation you have given your child!

$500 from Baby Shower

$500 from Parents

$500 from Four Grandparents ($2,000)

$3,000 invested at birth @ 15% compounded annually

VALUE AT	TOTAL INVESTED	PRINCIPAL/INTEREST
Age 18	$3,000	$37,126
Age 30	$3,000	$198,635
Age 40	$3,000	$803,590
Age 45	$3,000	$1,616,307
Age 50	$3,000	$3,250,972

My Definition of Retirement
To do what you want, when you want, how you want, and have the money to do it.

You Are on Your Own

The reality is—the responsibility for retirement planning has shifted from employers and the government to each of us. If you follow the ideas in this book, you can be wealthy along the way and throughout your long retirement life. Choose to reach retirement with enough finances. Have you stopped to think how long you will be in the glorious life of retirement at the fantastic age of 45?

Medical science and the United States census bureau have stated that a female at age 60, without any signs of cancer or heart problems, has a life span of 95 years. This means that your retirement could last 50 years! Now I call that awesome! Especially if you take care of your health so you can enjoy life to the fullest.

Imagine you and your beautiful wife, so young at 45, able to enjoy each other to the fullest. As stated in Chapter 1, this involves love-intimacy and financial-intimacy to reach your goals.

Chapter 5 shows you how to be worth $10 million 20 years from your wedding. This will give you $1 million income per year at 10% annual return (minus inflation and taxes) for life, plus be able to give the $10 million principal to your heirs and favorite charities at your death. This is the way to make your money last forever.

I would give anything to be able to start my life over at age 16, knowing what I know now. I learned so many things the hard way, which is one major reason for this book. In fact, I would have paid $1 million back then for this book you are reading.

> *The best gift you can give your children, grandchildren,*
> *nieces, nephews, and friends is a copy of this book.*
> *It would be like giving them each $10 million.*

My wish is that you, your children, and your grandchildren can avoid the mistakes I made. Learn early to make your money work hard for you rather than you working hard for your money. That way you can know you'll have the money you need to live your life fully, with plenty left over to give away.

The number one fear of retirees is to run out of money before they run out of life. This is happening today to millions who did not plan, save, and invest for the most important part of their life.

It's so sad to see seniors increasing their credit card and other debt at a time in life when they should be debt-free and rich. Current studies show that many seniors are defined as "debt hardship," those who pay 40% or more of their income to debt. They are still making other people millionaires with the high interest rather than being debt-free.

Put into practice the contents of this book, and you can live financially free. Read again the story of Arkad, the richest man in Babylon in Chapter 2.

Mistakes Made with Retirement Savings

- Failure to consider long-term care needs. More later.
- Failure to consider the effects of inflation and taxes. More later.
- Failure to take advantage of the years immediately before retirement.
- Make large loans to family and friends. This is a No No!
- Overestimating how much you can withdraw from your nest egg each year.
    With my plan, it should be zero while you still make money with your investments in retirement.
- Underestimating life-expectancy.
    Plan your finances as if you will live to 95 or 100. Did you know that the fastest growing age group in the country is the 100-year age group? In fact, for several decades the number has doubled. Follow the ideas in this book so you will have enough money for you and also be able to leave a legacy to your heirs and favorite charities.
- Underestimating expenses in retirement.
    People say you will need between 60%-80% of your last year's income to live comfortably in retirement. This is incorrect. These people are not retired—so how do they know? I am, and I can tell you that it takes more money to live in retirement than when I was working. Many friends say the same thing. Remember, retirement is doing what you want, when you want, and how you want. And that takes money.
- Focus only on your nest egg to the exclusion of all else.

Multiple Ongoing Streams of Income

It is important to have the money to spend when you need it. Create multiple, ongoing streams of income for life.

INCOME STREAMS	Total	10% Annual Return	15% Annual Return	Refer to pg #
Income Streams NOW				
$25,000 Cash Cushion FOR EMERGENCIES HAVE A HOME EQUITY LINE OF CREDIT	$25,000	$2,500	$3,750	112
Tax-free Income from sale OF APPRECIATED HOME (IF MARRIED)	$500,000	$50,000	$75,000	85
TOTAL Yearly Income		**$52,500**	**$78,750**	
Income Streams COMPOUNDED for 20 years				
401(k) $1,250 per month EMPLOYEE AND EMPLOYER CONTRIBUTION	$1,889,888	$188,988	$283,483	52
Reduced Income Taxes	$1,104,470	$110,447	$165,670	50
Interest-only home mortgage TAX SAVINGS ($8,000/YR) LOWER PAYMENT ($500/MO)	$942,481 $757,977	$94,248 $75,797	$141,372 $113,696	80/82 80/82
Creampuff used car versus new	$489,653	$48,965	$73,447	106
High school prom savings ($1,000)	$8,138	$813	$1,220	118
Income Tax Refund INVESTED/COMPOUNDED SEMIMONTHLY	$302,382	$30,238	$45,357	55/56
$200 saved per month INVESTED/COMPOUNDED ANNUALLY	$265,415	$26,541	$39,812	26
Invest twice monthly versus annually (FREE MONEY) ($200/MO VS $2,400/YR)	$36,967	$3,696	$5,545	52/53
TOTAL Yearly Income		**$579,733**	**$869,602**	
Income Stream COMPOUNDED beginning at Birth				
Birth to 45	$15,814,289	$1,581,428	$2,372,144	97
TOTAL Yearly Income		**$1,581,428**	**$2,372,144**	

Additional sources of ongoing income:
- Invest twice a month instead of once a year.
  Do this with all investments if possible—it's free money!
- Other retirement plans
- Securities
- Other investments
- Social Security
- American Cash Flow Corporation had training classes for 64 different income streams (see Resources)

Continue to Build Your Estate, Even in Retirement

Once you reach your retirement as a multimillionaire, do not assume you are going to discontinue your good investments. It is important to continue building your nest egg even in retirement. Why?
- Expected life span of 95 to 100 years of age
- Many retirees will be in retirement as long as their working years or longer (especially if you follow this book)
- It's easy to underestimate retirement income needs
- Inflation averaged 4% since 1934
- Increased medical costs
- Little or no Social Security
- Little or no Medicare
- Reduce welfare and medical coverage
- So you will not *have* to go back to work

Your Money Is Being Embezzled—By Inflation

Definition of inflation: "A persistent increase in the level of consumer prices or a persistent decline in the purchasing power of money, caused by an increase in available currency and credit beyond the proportion of available goods and services."

Many people do not give inflation a second thought as they plan for retirement. Do not bury your head in the sand. Over time, the price of most goods, services, and products goes up.

In periods of inflation, it takes more money to purchase the same goods and services. In fact, since 1934, inflation has increased prices an average of

4% per year. This means that a year from now you will pay 4% more for the same item you purchase today. So, if you spend $10 today, it will cost $10.40 a year from now and $10.82 the following year. Inflation can be very hard on anyone with low, fixed incomes. Inflation is all the more reason you need your investments working for you until you die.

Let's take $1 in 1940 and look at how the value has decreased over time. See how much money is needed to buy what $1 bought in 1940.

Another example is an item that cost $100 in 1980 cost $237.01 in 2005.

YEAR	VALUE	$ NEEDED TO = $1 IN 1940
1940	$1.00	$1.00
1950	$ .58	$1.72
1960	$ .48	$2.11
1970	$ .38	$2.77
1980	$ .19	$5.89
1990	$ .11	$9.34
2000	$ .08	$12.30
2005	$ .07	$13.95

Invest in Long-Term Care Insurance

Even your sizeable estate can be decimated with the current high cost of long-term care. Years ago my dad was in a long-term care facility for 11 years and three months. Can you imagine the total cost at today's rates?

Long-term care insurance is expensive, yet far less detrimental to your estate. Please consider the following reasons to invest in it.

- **You will be independent.**
  Not dependent on your family or the government for your care.
- **Protect the assets you have.**
  The U.S. Department of Labor estimates the average annual cost of nursing-home care in the next 30 years will be $190,000 a year.
- **Be able to select quality home care and/or quality assisted living/residential facility in a location of your own choosing.**
  Medicaid will place you wherever there is a bed, even if it's outside your local area.

- You maintain personal control and independence over the choices that need to be made for your care.
- You won't be an emotional or financial burden to your spouse or your children.
- You will maintain your dignity and have peace of mind.

Before you start thinking about long-term insurance, I recommend you read the free small booklet *Dignity For Life, Facts That Can Protect Your Assets and Quality of Life* (see Resources).

Many parents say they do not want to put the burden of long-term care on their children. Long-term care insurance allows you to maintain your own independence while knowing that the burden of this care will not fall on your family. Most seniors also realize that, by acquiring long-term care coverage—they are protecting the very assets that will some day go to their loved ones and favorite charities.

When discussing long-term care insurance with your children, remind them that out of love for them and respect for yourself, you want to insure a positive future for everyone. The best approach is to tell them that this insurance will help them to take care of you, and will protect family assets.

Most children feel their parents will never need long-term care. They imagine that if and when the time comes that their parents will need this kind of care, they will step in. Many times, when asked about this type of coverage, they will respond, "No, Mom/Dad, you will never go to a nursing home! We will take care of you." Out of love and obligation, it is difficult for them to imagine anything else.

They don't realize that it will be especially difficult for them to care for you if they are working full-time, and/or raising a family of their own. Although their intentions are good, the reality is that caring for a loved one 24 hours a day, seven days a week, month after month usually takes professional help. In most cases where children attempt to give long-term care to their parents, they soon come to realize that it is impossible for them to do it on their own. Only too late do they understand they should have encouraged their parents to purchase some kind of insurance. It is only then they see that the much-needed money for help is not there.

> *Your children do not yet comprehend*
> *the reality of long-term care situations.*

Summary

$ Retirement planning starts at birth. Follow the baby's growth estate plan and your child will be worth $1,616,307 at age 45—a perfect age to retire.

$ Teach your children to be financially independent at a young age by getting part-time work with a saving and investment plan. Many parents have to work until they die because they taught their children to be dependent on them throughout their life.

$ Teach your children to work their way through high-school and college. The $200,000 per child used to pay college expenses is better applied to your financial freedom. See Chapter 10.

$ Your college-age children could complete college debt-free (with no student loans) and a $300,000 net worth. See Chapter 10.

$ Pay cash. Remember, the only interest you should ever pay should be investment interest.

$ Enjoy life. **And save** to invest.

$ Compound your estate every 4.8 years at 15% investment return.

$ Reduce your taxes and invest for yourself.

$ Wait six years after marriage to have children.

$ Wife works first six years of marriage, and invest 100% of the one salary. See Chapter 5.

$ Purchase your own home and become a multimillionaire whether it's paid for or not. See Chapter 9.

$ Remember to avoid credit card debt because it costs you 145% interest per year. See Chapter 7.

$ Have all the pension plans possible. Start with a 401(k). It returns 100% per year interest year after year. See Chapter 5.

$ Follow as many of other ideas in this book as possible as you enjoy life while working toward becoming wealthy while young. Great success to you.

Resources
Book
The New Rules of Retirement by Bob Carlson

Bob Carlson's *Retirement Watch*
800-552-1152
retirementwatch.com

Free retirement material
T. Rowe Price   troweprice.com
Vanguard   vanguard.com

Inflation
inflationdata.com
westegg.com/inflation/
minneapolisfed.org/Research/data/us/calc/

Income stream trainings
American Cash Flow Corporation
800-713-6901
americancashflow.com/

Internal Revenue Service
irs.gov
Publication 590, Individual Retirement Arrangements (IRA)
minimum distributions and life expectancy tables
Publication 575, Pension and Annuity Income
for 410(k) minimum distribution rules and rollover rules
Publication 560, Retirement Plans for Small Business
SEP, SIMPLE, and Qualified Plans

Publication 571, Tax-Sheltered Annuity Plans
    403(b) plans
Publication 564, Mutual Fund Distributions
      for calculating cost basis, required minimum distribution
      rules, RMD calculator, and planning tips

Long-term Care Insurance
   Free booklet
      Dignity For Life, Facts That Can Protect Your Assets and Quality of Life
      916-961-8107
      ltcfp.us/SandraStanley
         Create a tailor-made policy to meet your needs.

Almost anyone can retire in style
by planting a little seed capital many years in advance.
The primary secret to wealth creation is time.
If you retire before you're rich,
you may live a life of leisure and reasonable security—
provided you die suddenly, and soon.

Chapter 18 | *You Can Become a Millionaire Even If You Start Late*

Wow! One morning you wake up and say to yourself, "I forgot to get rich so I can retire with wealth. Now what do I do?" This is the time in life to pull out all the stops and go 90 miles an hour to make up for lost time.

You do not want to be like the couple whose financial advisor said he had good news for them. It was one of those good-news-bad-news stories. "The good news," he said, "is you are going to have all the money you need to have a great retirement." They reply, "That is wonderful. What's the bad news?" The advisor says, "Both of you will have to work until you are 85 years old."

Please, listen carefully. Get this book in the hands of your children and grandchildren so they can immediately begin to create their financial freedom.

Now, back to helping you become a millionaire. You will need to make some sacrifices, and it can be done. If married, you and your spouse must work together very closely and quickly to make it happen.

I was fascinated by a quiz I read in a recent *Kiplinger Retirement Report*.

Question One—"To retire comfortably and securely, you must accumulate $1 million by age sixty-five. True or false?"
Answer One— "True, and actually you may need more."

Question Two—"Approximately eighty-nine percent of all Americans will depend on help from their family and/or the government to support them in retirement. True or false?"
Answer Two—"False. It is ninety-six percent."

Question Three—"Will you and your children be one of the ninety-six percent or will you be in the four percent group?"

Do you choose to be in the 4%?

Are You 10 Years from Retirement?

If so, scale down expenses rapidly. If married, live on one salary and invest 100% of the second. There are many books on how to live on one salary and still enjoy life. The ones in the library are free.

Assume the one salary you invest is $35,000 per year. This plus your home value, Social Security, and savings should make you a millionaire.

Year	$ Invested	@15% Interest	Balance
1	$35,000	$5,250	$40,250
2	$35,000	$11,288	$86,538
3	$35,000	$18,231	$139,768
4	$35,000	$26,215	$200,983
5	$35,000	$35,398	$271,381
6	$35,000	$45,957	$352,338
7	$35,000	$58,101	$445,439
8	$35,000	$72,066	$552,504
9	$35,000	$88,126	$675,630
10	$35,000	$106,595	$817,225

If You Are Not Financially Ready

$ Get out of debt quickly and avoid interest payments. Remember, you are paying interest that makes others millionaires while you grovel along in debt. Cut up your credit cards.

$ Find the money to start saving and investing. See Chapter 3.

$ Make saving and investing automatic. The ultimate would be your 401(k) investment. Automatically have your payroll department withhold from your paycheck each pay period and have it go directly into your 401(k) account.

$ Increase your contributions to your 401(k) pension until you have reached the maximum allowed. If your employer has a matching plan, this will give you a 100% return. Each spouse can stash up to $15,000 per year in his or her employers 401(k) plan or $20,000 per year if over age 50.

$ Once you have reached your maximum on your 401(k) or 403(b), start funding other pension plans.

$ Start a home-based business for added income and hundreds of legal tax deductions.

$ Hire your children, if they are still at home.

$ Take a second job or work extra hours.

$ Sell non-producing, unused, or rarely used items and invest the profits.

$ Question every single penny you spend and ask yourself, "Am I purchasing a luxury or a necessity, a need or want?" Invest the difference.

$ See Appendix for *2000 Ways to Lower Living Expenses.*

$ Save money by eliminating or reducing seldom-used monthly fees. For example, 15 million people still rent their phones and the average family watches only 15 TV channels, so why pay for hundreds?

$ If you use a line phone, Internet, and cable television, consider the new competitive 3-in-1 plans and reduce your monthly costs.

$ If your current life insurance policy is three to five years old, review and receive the same coverages at a reduced rate and invest the savings.

$ Get comparative bids on your house, car, and earthquake insurance and all major purchases.

$ Purchase a creampuff, low-mileage used automobile from friend, co-worker, acquaintance, etc. Save $4,000 per year versus a new car.

$ Cancel private mortgage insurance.

$ Become a millionaire from home ownership. See Chapter 9.

$ Rent out a room.

$ Sell your appreciated home and have up to $500,000 totally and absolutely tax free. Purchase a less expensive home and invest the rest. You can do this every two years if you live in a fast-appreciating area.

$ Reduce your income tax legally and invest. See Chapter 13.

$ See Appendix for *2000 Ways to Lower Income Tax* and invest what you save.

$ Invest in income producing real estate. See Chapter 15.

$ Make bill paying automatic. Have your bank pay them monthly and free up your time.

$ If any of your children age 21 or older live at home and have an income, require them to pay a monthly contribution to cover the cost of room, meals, utilities, laundry, insurance, taxes, etc. In other words, **charge them rent**.

$ Stay clear of annuities and insurance policies that require a large up-front commission.

$ Remember all the other ways mentioned throughout this book to save and/or make money to invest.

$ Put off retirement to age 65 or 70, if absolutely necessary.

Become a Millionaire During Retirement

If you are retired and would still love to become a millionare, choose two or three of the following ways. These ideas are not pie in the sky. I have used every one during periods of my life and currently use several in semi-retirement. First educate yourself on finances.

$ Spend one hour a month and follow the buy and sell recommendations from top financial newsletters.

$ Begin a home-based business for additional income and tax savings.

$ Get out of debt, and then invest. See Chapter 8.

$ Review the 80 ways to become a millionaire. All you need is two or three that do not affect your lifestyle. See Chapter 11.

$ Reduce or eliminate income tax and invest the savings. See Chapter 13.

$ Compound your investment returns. See Chapter 2.

$ Continue with the good investments that you currently have.

$ Purchase carefully selected stocks.

$ Use leverage every way possible.

$ Purchase your home or refinance existing mortgage using interest-only loans. See Chapter 9.

$ Invest in well-located, carefully selected real estate with a positive monthly cash flow—rental homes, multi-family apartments, business property, etc.

$ Purchase, repair, and sell two to three run down homes each year and make $100,000 a year. In 10 years you'll have $1 million.

$ Sell unneeded life insurance policies for more money than the cash surrender value and invest.

Even term-life insurance policies qualify if they can be converted to universal-life or whole-life. Get three bids.

$ Finance factoring or accounts receivable.

A small business needs cash flow and is willing to take a discount on their accounts receivable to have the money now. You pay them 80% of the total invoice and then 30-60 days later the invoice is paid directly to you and you make 20% profit. Keep 5% invested for bad debt and have a 15% return. You can invest any amount of money you desire. I did this for years and made 100%-150% a year with little risk. Find the companies by placing an ad in the money to loan section of your local newspaper.

$ Purchase trust deeds at a discount.

Many holders of trust deeds are happy to convert a 2- to 10-year trust deed into cash **now**. Place an ad in your local newspaper stating "Money available to purchase trust deeds for cash at a discount." Offer a 20%-50% discount. You will receive the monthly payments, including the interest rate and full amount stipulated on the deed, for the duration of the deed.

I don't know your age, but I do know that you can choose today to take control of your finances. Remember, there are lots of possibilities if you focus on what you want. Whether you chose to become a millionaire, or to create an increased cash flow so that you have a few more options, you can do it if you think you can. I trust you will find hope in this book, hope that **you can** create the financial life you choose.

Resources

Book

Retire Rich and Young by Robert Kiyosaki

Newsletters and Reports

Bob Carlson's *Retirement Watch Newsletter*
800-915-5627

Free Retirement Plan Pocket Guide
Pioneer Investment Management, Inc.,
800-622-0181 or 800-225-6292
Ask for literature department.

Kiplinger's Retirement Report
800-419-0426
I have subscribed for years and find every issue beneficial.

The Hulbert Financial Digest
866-428-6568
This newsletter rates all the other financial newsletters.
Ask for a free sample.

> *When it comes to money,*
> *the only person you can count on is yourself.*

Chapter 19 | *Positive Financial Surprises— Finding Lost Assets*

Some $500 million in lost assets are unclaimed every year in my state of California. And more than $35 billion are "lost" and unclaimed each year nationwide. Yes, you read that right, "b" as in billion. In addition, hundreds of billions of dollars in IRS and Social Security checks are uncashed. You ask, "Who's losing their assets?" Would you believe—it's 80% of all Americans over the age of 19!

What Is a Lost Asset?

The National Association of Unclaimed Property Administrators (NAUPA) says this, "Unclaimed property (sometimes referred to as abandoned) refers to accounts in financial institutions and companies that have had no activity generated or contact with the owner for one year or a longer period."

I find it very hard to understand why people allow some of their hard-earned money to become lost forever.

Let me give you a few examples:

- After hearing this at one of my seminars, a 30-year-old decided to see for himself. He was shocked when he found that a $500,000 legacy had been left to him. Relatives had known about it for years, and out of anger had not told him.
- A very dear friend of mine, after being alerted by another friend, received a $71,000 check in the mail from the state unclaimed department. He had purchased stock in a company years ago that had gone belly up. Later, someone purchased the company, made a go of it, and paid off the former stockholders.

- Michael Finney, a newsman for the ABC affiliate in Los Angeles, did a segment on unclaimed property. He took his laptop to an L.A. street corner and randomly stopped people. He typed their names into the California Web site to check, and would you believe 80% of the people had unclaimed property!

- In Florida, a person who purchased a lottery ticket allowed the 180-day deadline to pass. (I hope you are sitting down!) The person who purchased the winning ticket lost $50 million! Why a person would go through the trouble of purchasing a lottery ticket and not follow up? Here's another shocker. The Florida lottery officials said it was the largest of **19** unclaimed jackpots in the past 15 years. Yes, you read that correctly, 19 gigantic unclaimed jackpots. And this is only one state!

- In New Jersey, a $23.7 million lottery prize went unclaimed because the winner didn't produce the ticket within the one-year deadline.

The Most Common Lost Assets

Securities make up the largest category of the hundreds of types of lost and unclaimed assets. Why? Very simple. Not keeping current records of every single asset.

More than $13.5 billion are lost in unredeemed savings bonds alone. In addition, once a bond matures, 30 or 40 years after purchase, the interest stops. Consequently, there's a lot of interest not being earned on $13.5 billion! How does this happen?

Bonds were popular in 1950s and 1960s. The original purchasers are now old. They forget that they have the bonds and then they die. Their busy grown children fly home for the funeral and have only a few days to empty the house, list it with a realtor, and return home. They generally rent a large Dumpster and into it goes 70, 80, or 90 years of records and collections, along with the bonds and other important legal documents.

To make matters worse, the children could be in trouble when the IRS comes knocking on their door wondering where the bonds are? And there may be a tax bill for all the accrued interest earned since the bond was purchased (way back when) plus penalties, late fees, etc.

You see, the government does not send out statements to bondholders. Many people sitting on fortunes do not realize it until it is too late!

Finally, I want to mention utilities. Even though the amounts are generally under $200, if you have two or three it adds up. Did you know this is one of the top five of all lost and unclaimed properties? Why? Very simple, you lost track of the deposit, moved, and forgot to get the refund. Some people make this one mistake over and over again.

Common Types of Forgotten and Lost Assets

- Annuities
- Bank accounts, savings or checking
- Bonds
- Certificates of deposit
- Closely held corporations controlled by deceased
- Customer overpayments
- Estates
- Health insurance reimbursements
- Hidden money
- Income tax refunds
- Inheritances, all types
- Individual Retirement Accounts (IRAs)
- Insurance payments or refunds
- Life insurance policies
- Loans receivable
- Mineral royalty payments
- Pension funds
- Real estate
- Refunds
- Safe deposit box contents
- Stocks, brokerage accounts, and REITs
- Traveler's checks
- Trust distributions
- Uncashed dividend or payroll checks

- Unredeemed money orders or gift certificates (in some states)
- Utility security deposits

How Did My Assets Become Lost?

All 50 states take the same position: they are not your baby sitter. It's not their business to keep track of every asset of every citizen. We, you and I, create the problem. If we each kept track of our assets, there would be no problem.

Each state has laws that requires banks, security companies, savings and loans, insurance companies, etc. to close an account and send all of your money to the state controller's office unclaimed property division. In California, if these companies have not had contact with you in three years, the law says you have only three more years to reclaim your property. If you do not reclaim it, you have lost your money or assets forever. Every year California puts hundreds of millions of dollars in unclaimed money into their general fund.

- Procrastination is the number one reason.
- You do not keep track of your assets, including all utility deposits.
- You move and fail to send address changes. Mail is forwarded for only one year.
- Notices are ignored. The institution assumes that you are lost after three years.
- Unused bank accounts, which remain dormant without contact, are automatically sent to the state.
- Some people plain forget about their assets.
- The older one becomes, the more assets are lost and forgotten.
- Many people die and do not leave good records.

What Happens to Lost Assets?

All 50 states have different laws regarding unclaimed assets. As stated earlier, in California, there is a six-year window then the unclaimed assets are gone forever. Some states hold onto unclaimed assets for five years; others hold them permanently.

Contact your state unclaimed-property department and ask about its policy. At the end of this chapter, to make it easy for you, I have included an alphabetical list by state with the department to contact, address, phone number(s), and Web site address. Thie list was accurate when this book went to print.

Remember, many states eventually put unclaimed assets in their general fund and the money is lost forever.

Reclaim Your Lost Assets

Unclaimed assets can be a small utility deposit, to the $50 million unclaimed lottery ticket. Some people are so irresponsible that they forget to apply for their own retirement plans. The administrator of a nationwide hotel chain said that 50% of those who leave their employment fail to claim their retirement income. You are beginning to see how unclaimed assets amount to **$35 billion lost each year**. How much is yours?

The important question is, "How can I get my lost asset back before, in some states, it is lost forever?"

Use the alphabetical list at the end of this chapter to check with your state and every state you have ever lived in. Remember to check maiden names and nicknames. While you're at it, check for family members, friends, and relatives.

The site will not tell you what the lost asset is. The procedure is simply to reclaim lost assets. Once you have found money, then you file on the computer to request a simple form or call the unclaimed-property division in your state. Request the form, which they will mail to you. It is very short and simple. Fill it out, mail it in, and your check will arrive shortly.

Keep a Record of Your Assets

Create and maintain a current list of assets, where they are, when they come due, who, to contact, etc., and encourage your parents to do the same.

$ There is a free *Personal Family and Financial Record Book*.
Ordering information is listed under Resources. Please, please, take the time to fill it out. Record all of your assets and liabilities and other important information. Keep it current by recording when you buy or sell any

asset. Tell your spouse or trustee where you keep the completed information.

$ Create a net worth statement each year when you do your income taxes.

Give a copy to your spouse or trustee. Also, give updates during the year of any assets purchased or sold to keep them current. This will save your family from possible large losses at your death, and months of research trying to locate all of your assets.

$ Mail change of address notices when you move to all your banks, brokers, insurance, etc.

Use the list *Remember Your Assets* at the end of this chapter to remind you whom to send your change of address to.

$ Before you move, close all accounts and collect your money.
$ Collect all utility deposits.
$ Pay attention to notices from your bank, broker, etc.

In summary, keep your hard-earned money. Take the precautions in this chapter. Above all, act now! Your objective is to work smarter. And remember, you are not going to become a millionaire if you keep losing your assets! Much success.

Resources
Bonds
    treasurydirect.gov

Finding Lost Assets
    State List
        To make it easy for you, a state list is included in this chapter with department to contact, address, phone number(s), and Web site National Association of Unclaimed Property
        unclaimed.org
    missingmoney.com

Lost Income Tax Refunds
  irs.gov
      Use the "Where's My Refund?" feature on the home page
      800-829-1954 Refund Hotline

Pension Funds
  PBGC Pension Search Program
      1200 K Street NW, Suite 930, Washington, DC 20005-4026
      pbgc.gov

Recording Assets
  Free booklet *Personal Family and Financial Record Book*
      American Institute for Cancer Research,
          800-843-8114 or 202-328-7744 in District of Columbia
          aicr.org/site/Ecommerce?store_id=1301& VIEW_
              CATALOG

Safe Deposit Boxes
  Contact your state controller's office (see list by state)

Social Security Administration
  800-772-1213
  ssa.gov/
      Get your earnings records.
      Former employers' Federal ID number will be on your record.
  freeERISA.com
      Use past employers' ID number to search any pension funds.

> *When we do the best we can,*
> *we never know what miracle is wrought in our life,*
> *or in the life of another.*
> HELEN KELLER

State List

Alabama
Office of State Treasurer
Unclaimed Property Division
PO Box 302520
Montgomery, AL 36130-2520
334-242-9614
888-844-8400
treasury.state.al.us/website/ucpd/
ucpd_frameset.html

Alaska
State of Alaska
Tax Division
PO Box 110420
Juneau, AK 99811-0420
907-465-3726
tax.state.ak.us/UnclaimedProperty/

Arizona
Department of Revenue
Unclaimed Property Unit
PO Box 29026, Site Code 604
Phoenix, AZ 85038-9026
602-364-0380
azunclaimed.gov/

Arkansas
Unclaimed Property Division
Auditor of State
1400 West Third Street Suite 100
Little Rock, AR 72201-1811
501-682-6000 or 800-252-4648
claimit@auditorjimwood.org
state.ar.us/auditor/unclprop/

California
Division of Collections
Bureau of Unclaimed Property
PO Box 942850
Sacramento, CA 94250-5873
916-323-2827
800-992-4647 CA Residents
sco.ca.gov/col/ucp/

Colorado
Office of State Treasurer
Unclaimed Property Division
1120 Lincoln Street, Suite 1004
Denver, CO 80203
303-894-2443 or 800-825-2111
colorado.gov/treasury/gcp/index.html

Connecticut
Office of the State Treasurer
Unclaimed Property Division
PO Box 5065
Hartford, CT 06102
800-833-7318
ctbiglist.com/

Delaware
Dept. of Finance, Division of Revenue
State Escheator
PO Box 8931
Wilmington, DE 19801-3509
302-577-8220
state.de.us/revenue/information/
Escheat.shtml

District of Columbia
DC Office of Finance and Treasury
Unclaimed Property Unit
810 1st Street, NE, Suite 401
Washington, DC 20002
202-442-8181
dcunclaimed.property@dc.gov
cfo.dc.gov/cfo/cwp/view,a,
1326,q,590614,cfoNav,%7C33208
%7C.asp

Florida
Florida Dept. of Financial Services
Unclaimed Property Bureau
200 E. Gaines Street
Tallahassee, FL 32399-0358
850-413-5555 or 888-258-2253
850-413-3017 fax
funclaim@fldfs.com
fltreasurehunt.org/

Georgia
Georgia Department of Revenue
Local Government Services-
   Unclaimed Property
4245 International Parkway, Suite A
Hapeville, GA 30354-3918
404-968-0490
404-968-0772 fax
ucpmail@dor.ga.gov
etax.dor.ga.gov/ptd/ucp/index.shtml

Guam
Treasurer of Guam
PO Box 884
Agana, GU 96910

Hawaii
Department of Budget and Finance
Unclaimed Property Program
PO Box 150
Honolulu, HI 96810
unclaimedproperty@hawaii.gov
hawaii.gov/budget/uncprop/

Idaho
State Tax Commission
Unclaimed Property Program
PO Box 70012
Boise, ID 83707-0112
208-334-7627 or 800-972-7660
lostandfound@tax.idaho.gov
tax.idaho.gov/unclaimed.htm

Illinois
Office of State Treasurer
Unclaimed Property Division
PO Box 19495
Springfield, IL 62794-9495
217-785-6992
866-458-7327 IL Residents
cashdash.net/

Indiana
Office of the Attorney General
Unclaimed Property Division
PO Box 2504
Greenwood, IN 46142
866.462.5246
upd@atg.state.in.us
in.gov/attorneygeneral/ucp/

Iowa
Great Iowa Treasure Hunt
Lucas State Office Building
321 E. 12th St., 1st Floor.
Des Moines, IA 50319
515-281-5367
foundit@tos.state.ia.us
greatiowatreasurehunt.com/

Kansas
Kansas State Treasurer
Unclaimed Property Division
900 SW Jackson, Suite 201
Topeka, KS 66612-1235
785-296-4165 or 800-432-0386
800-432-0386 KS Residents
785-291-3172 fax
unclaimed@treasurer.state.ks.us
kansasstatetreasurer.com/prodweb/up/

Kentucky
Kentucky State Treasury
Unclaimed Property Division
1050 US Highway 127 South, Suite 100
Frankfort, KY 40601
800-465-4722
502-564-4200 fax
unclaimed.property@ky.gov
kytreasury.com/

Louisiana
Office of the State Treasurer
Unclaimed Property Division
PO Box 91010
Baton Rouge, LA 70821-9010
225-219-9400 or 888-925-4127
treasury.state.la.us/

Maine
State Treasurer's Office
Unclaimed Property Division
39 State House Station
Augusta, ME 04333
207-624-7470
888-283-2808 ME Residents
unclaimed.property@maine.gov
maine.gov/treasurer/unclaimed_
property/

Maryland
Comptroller of Maryland
Unclaimed Property Unit
301 W. Preston Street
Baltimore, MD 21201-2385
410-767-1700 or 800-782-7383
interactive.marylandtaxes.com/
Individuals/Unclaim/default.aspx

Massachusetts
Department of the State Treasurer
Abandoned Property Division
One Ashburton Place, 12th Floor
Boston, MA 02108-1608
617-367-0400
800-647-2300 MA Residents
abpweb.tre.state.ma.us/abp/abp.htm

Michigan
Office of the State Treasurer
Unclaimed Property Division
Lansing, MI 48922
517-636-5320
517-636-5324 fax
michigan.gov/treasury/0,1607,7-121-
1748_1876_1912-7924--,00.html

Minnesota
Minnesota Dept. of Commerce
Unclaimed Property Program
85 7th Place East, Suite 500
St. Paul, MN 55101-2198
651-296-2568
800-925-5668 MN Residents
state.mn.us/portal/mn/jspcontentdo?id
=-536881373&agency=Commerce

Mississippi
Mississippi Treasury
Unclaimed Property Division
PO Box 138
Jackson, MS 39205
601-359-3600
treasury.state.ms.us/Unclaimed/

Missouri
State Treasurer's Office
Unclaimed Property Section
P.O. Box 1004
Jefferson City, MO 65102-1272
573-751-0840
ucp@treasurer.mo.gov
treasurer.mo.gov/mainUCP.asp

Montana
Department of Revenue
Attn: Unclaimed Property
PO Box 5805
Helena, MT 59604-5805
406-444-6900
406-444-0722 fax
UnclaimedProperty@mt.gov
mt.gov/revenue/programsandservices/
unclaimedproperty.asp

Nebraska
Office of the State Treasurer
Unclaimed Property Division
PO Box 94788
Lincoln, NE 68509
402-471-2455
treasurer.state.ne.us/ie/uphome.asp

Nevada
Office of the State Treasurer
Unclaimed Property Division
555 E Washington Ave., Suite 4200
Las Vegas, NV 89101-1070
702-486-4140
800-521-0019 NV Residents
nevadatreasurer.gov/unclaimed/

New Hampshire
Treasury Department
Unclaimed Property Division
25 Capitol Street, Room 205
Concord, NH 03301
603-271-2619
800-791-0920 NH Residents
nh.gov/treasury/Divisions/AP/
  APindex.htm

New Jersey
Office of the State Treasurer
Unclaimed Property
PO Box 214
Trenton, NJ 08695-0214
609-292-9200
state.nj.us/treasury/taxation/index.
  html?updisel.htm - mainFrame

New Mexico
Taxation & Revenue Department
Unclaimed Property Division
PO Box 25123
Santa Fe, NM 87504-5123
505-476-1774
uproperty@state.nm.us
https://ec3.state.nm.us/ucp/

New York
Office of the State Comptroller
Office of Unclaimed Funds
110 State Street, 8th Floor
Albany, NY 12236
518-270-2200
800-221-9311 NY Residents
wwe1.osc.state.ny.us/ouf/ouf
  SearchForm.html

North Carolina
Department of State Treasurer
Unclaimed Property Program
325 North Salisbury Street
Raleigh, NC 27603-1385
919-508-1000
919-508-5181 fax
unclaimed.property@treasurer.state.
  nc.us
https://www.nctreasurercomDstHome/
  AdminServicesUnclaimedProperty/
  Search.htm

North Dakota
State Land Department
Unclaimed Property Division
PO Box 5523
Bismarck, ND 58506-5523
701.328.2800
llfisher@state.nd.us
land.state.nd.us/

Ohio
Department of Commerce
Division of Unclaimed Funds
77 South High Street, 20th floor
Columbus, OH 43215-6108
614-466-4433
unclaimedfundstreasurehunt.ohio.gov/

Oklahoma
Oklahoma State Treasurer
Unclaimed Property Division
4545 N. Lincoln Blvd., Ste. 106
Oklahoma City, OK 73105-3413
405-521-4273
unclaimed@treasurer.ok.gov
https://www.ok.gov/unclaimed/index.
  php

Oregon
Division of State Lands
Trust Property Section
775 Summer St. NE #100
Salem, OR 97301-1279
503-378-3805
oregon.gov/DSL/index.shtml

Pennsylvania
State Treasurer
Unclaimed Property Division
PO Box 1837
Harrisburg, PA 17105-1837
800-222-2046
patreasury.org/

Puerto Rico
Office of the Commissioner of
    Financial Inst.
Alfredo Padilla, Commissioner
PO Box 11855
San Juan, PR 00910-3855
787-723-3131
cif.gov.prunclaimedeng/
    unclaimedmain.aspx

Rhode Island
Office of the General Treasurer
Unclaimed Property Division
PO Box 1435
Providence, RI 02901
401-222-6505
ups@treasury.state.ri.us
treasury.state.ri.usmoneylst.htm

South Carolina
Unclaimed Property Program
State Treasurer's Office
PO Box 11778
Columbia, SC 29211
803-737-4771
803-734-2668 fax
payback@sto.state.sc.us
state.sc.us/treas/

South Dakota
Office of the State Treasurer
Unclaimed Property Division
500 East Capitol Ave, Suite 212
Pierre, SD 57501-5070
605-773-3379
sdtreasurer.com/

Tennessee
Treasury Department
Unclaimed Property Division
Andrew Jackson Bldg., 9th Floor
500 Deaderick Street
Nashville, TN 37243-0242
615-741-6499
treasury.state.tn.us/unclaim/

Texas
Comptroller of Public Accounts
Unclaimed Property Division
PO Box 12019
Austin, TX 78711-2019
800-654-FIND (3463)
unclaimed.property@cpa.state.tx.us
https://txcpa.cpa.state.tx.us/up/Search.
    jsp

Utah
State Treasurer's Office
Unclaimed Property Division
341 South Main St., 5th Floor
Salt Lake City, UT 84111
801-320-5360 or 888-217-1203
up.state.ut.us/

Vermont
Vermont State Treasurer
Abandoned Property Division
Pavillion Building
109 State Street, 4th Floor
Montpelier, VT 05609-6200
802-828-2407
800-642-3191 VT Residents
vermonttreasurer.gov/

Virgin Islands
Office of the Lieutenant Governor
Division of Banking
18 Kongens Gade
St. Thomas, VI 00802

Virginia

Virginia Department of the Treasury
Division of Unclaimed Property
PO Box 2478
Richmond, VA 23218-2478
804-225-2393 or 800-468-1088
ucpmail@trs.virginia.gov
trs.virginia.gov/ucp/ucp.asp

Washington

Department of Revenue
Unclaimed Property Section
PO Box 47477
Olympia, WA 98504-7477
360-705-6706
800-435-2429 WA Residents
ucp.dor.wa.gov/

West Virginia

Office of the State Treasurer
Unclaimed Property Division
One Players Club Drive
Charleston, WV 25305
304-558-2937 or 800-642-8687
wvsto.com/

Wisconsin

State Treasurer's Office
Unclaimed Property Division
PO Box 2114
Madison, WI 53701-2114
608-267-7977
unclaim@ost.state.wi.us
ost.state.wi.us/home/unclaim.htm

Wyoming

Office of the State Treasurer
Unclaimed Property
2515 Warren Avenue, Suite 502
Cheyenne, WY 82002
307-777-5590
treasurer.state.wy.us/uphome.asp

Additional Resources for Unclaimed Money

Credit Union Shares
ncua.gov/AssetMgmtCent/unclaimed/
unclaimed.html

Dividend Checks
www2.fdic.gov/funds/index.asp

HUD Refunds
www.hud.gov/offices/hsg/comp/
refunds/index.cfm

Pension Benefits
https://www.pbgc.gov/Missing
Participant/missingParticipant
Search.jsp

Tax Refunds
irs.ustreas.gov

Canada and British Columbia
ucbswww.bank-banque-canada.ca
bcunclaimedproperty.bc.ca/

NOTE

This information is provided for your convenience
and was accurate when this book was printed.

Remember Your Assets

PERSONAL		RETIREMENT INCOME	
Checking Accounts	$_____	401(k)	$_____
Savings Accounts	$_____	Annuity Payments	$_____
Safe Deposit Box	$_____	Interest	$_____
Veteran's Benefits	$_____	IRA Income	$_____
Family Trust	$_____	Keogh Income	$_____
Automobiles	$_____	Pensions	$_____
Home	$_____	Social Security	$_____
Appliances	$_____	_____	$_____
Antiques	$_____	_____	$_____
Clothing	$_____	_____	$_____
Collectibles	$_____	_____	$_____
Computers	$_____	_____	$_____
Electronics	$_____	_____	$_____
Furniture	$_____		
Jewelry	$_____	INVESTMENT INCOME	
Paintings	$_____	Bond Interest	$_____
Tools	$_____	CDs	$_____
Second Home	$_____	Money Market Accnts	$_____
Business Interest	$_____	Mutual Fund Interest	$_____
Partnerships	$_____	Real Estate Income	$_____
Bonds	$_____	Stock Dividends	$_____
Stocks	$_____	Trust Deeds	$_____
Mutual Funds	$_____	_____	$_____
Life Insurance		_____	$_____
(cash value)	$_____	_____	$_____
Tax Refunds	$_____	_____	$_____
SocSec Burial Funds	$_____	_____	$_____
_____	$_____	_____	$_____
TOTAL Column 1	$_____	**TOTAL Column 2**	$_____
		GRAND TOTAL	$_____

| Chapter 20 | *Put More Money in Your Pocket Than You Give Away* |

Would you believe that being a philanthropist can put more money in your pocket than you actually give away? It's true! I'll give you some examples in this chapter.

First, let us look at the definition of philanthropy. According to Webster's Dictionary, *"Philanthropy is a desire to help mankind as by gifts to charitable or humanitarian institutions."* This can be your favorite church, synagogue, mosque, or charity—providing that it is a qualified nonprofit organization.

Did you know you can be a philanthropist by giving $10,000 or less to your favorite charity? You do not have to give millions of dollars to be a philanthropist; and it is great if you can.

If you have been following the suggestions in this book, you are going to have a sizeable estate. And what are you going to do with it? Remember there are only four options.

> Give it to your heirs.
> Give it to the government.
> Give it to your favorite charity.
> Or a combination of all three.

Before you say your farewells and climb into your casket, why not take the time to prepare a solid estate plan so that your wonderful legacy can live on and on after you. It takes only about two to three days. The majority of people don't leave behind even a simple will or living trust. Their families are then forced into a complicated, time-consuming nightmare of probate court.

Please, understand: If you work most of your life, 16 of those years will be just to pay taxes. Why don't you take a couple of days to plan your estate while you are still able? Remember, you cannot take care of or plan your estate if you have Alzheimer's, are on your death bed, or have passed away.

Here are some important statistics:

- 80% of all Americans do not even have a simple will.
- 90% of all Americans who need a living will do not have one.
- 53% of all affluent Americans do not have an estate plan in place (according to *USA Today*).
- 63% of all business owners do not have a succession plan.

There are three non-negotiable facts regarding your estate.

- You own stuff.
- You will die.
- Someone will get that stuff. Will it be the people you love?

> *Please make an appointment with an estate planning attorney or development officer of your favorite charity before going to bed tonight.*

Protect Your Assets

Choose to give your assets to your heirs and favorite charity rather than paying the bulk or all of your estate in taxes, court fees, attorney fees, and many other possible fees.

Make sure you are not part of the Triple Ninety rule.

90% of the time people who are
90 years old have
90% of their estate intact and have **no estate plan**

In Chapter 2 you learned about the miracle of compound interest. Now you are going to learn how to compound certain assets and your entire estate. That's right. Whether your estate is worth $10,000 or $10 million, you will see how easy it is to compound your estate multiple times, all while making money. "How is that possible?" you ask. Read on.

Gift Plan Models

The following 10 pages are illustrated gift plan models for you to consider as part of your overall estate transfer plan. The commentary on the illustrations was provided by W. Robert Daum, CSPG, a certified specialist in planned giving.

Remember, this information is not intended to provide advice for any specific situation. Advice from a qualified attorney and/or tax accountant should always be obtained before implementing any of the strategies described. The word "property" may refer to real estate, stocks, bonds, mutual funds, or other assets.

The income tax deductions are based on 6.2 AFR (Applicable Federal Rate), which is set each month according to IRS regulations.

Please note the tremendous compounding in addition to the substantial tax advantages.

We make a living by what we get,
but we make a life by what we give.
WINSTON S. CHURCHILL

Gift Annuity
$10,000 Cash Gift

At age 80, Mary's CDs are paying a low interest rate and she wishes to receive a higher rate. She writes a check for $10,000 as a gift to her favorite charity in exchange for a Life Income Annuity Agreement.

Mary immediately begins receiving $800 per year for life in quarterly payments of $200. For 10 years $511 will be tax-free, then it will all be taxable.

The charity invests Mary's gift during her lifetime. At the end of Mary's life, the charity will use the remaining gift in its mission as specified by Mary.

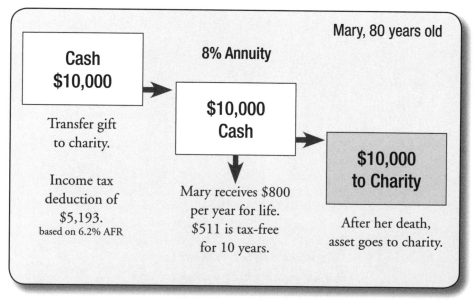

courtesy of W. Robert Daum, CSPG

Gift Annuity
$75,000 Property Gift

John's property (stocks or real estate) has appreciated and he would like a higher income with no management responsibilities. He transfers the property to his favorite charity as a gift in exchange for a Life Income Annuity Agreement.

At 76, John receives $5,400 each year in monthly installments. Part is tax-free income. He also enjoys the tax advantages of a partial bypass on the capital gains and may take a charitable income tax deduction of $36,904.

The charity sells the property and invests the money as long as John lives. Then it goes to work for the charity as directed by John in the annuity agreement.

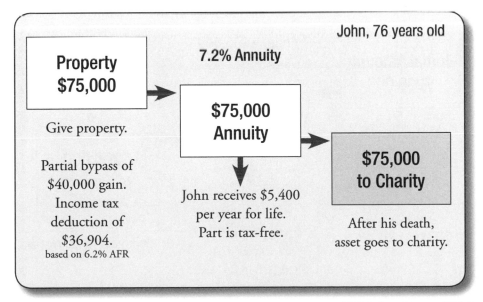

courtesy of W. Robert Daum, CSPG

Retirement Annuity
$200,000 Property Gift

At 45 years of age, John and Mary have made a successful investment which they would like to put away for future income. They transfer the $200,000 asset to their chosen charity as a gift in exchange for a Deferred Annuity Income Agreement.

They specify they would like the flexibility of electing to start the income at any time between the ages of 55 and 85. At their normal retirement age of 67, their annual income would be $35,600 or almost $3,000 every month for as long as either of them is living. At age 67, their life expectancy is 24 years which would give them an income of $811,998, more if they live longer.

All assets of the charity are pledged to pay them as promised. John and Mary also realize several income tax benefits now and part of the income is tax free for a term of years.

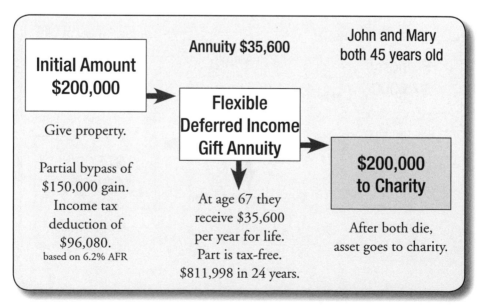

courtesy of W. Robert Daum, CSPG

Life Estate Reserved Gift
Home or Farm

If you like your home or farm where you live, you don't plan to move again, and you would like to give your property to your favorite charity—you may sign a deed transferring the property to the charity and specify in the deed your reservation of ownership rights as long as you live or elect to give up those rights.

The amount of your immediate income tax deduction is based on your age on the day you sign the deed. The deduction may be carried forward up to five additional years.

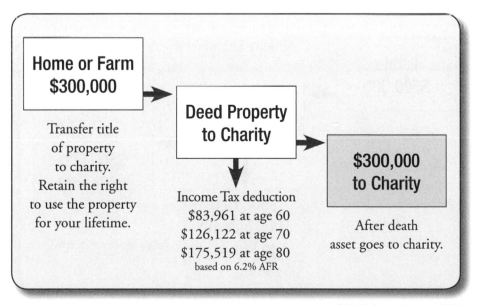

courtesy of W. Robert Daum, CSPG

"Give it Twice" Trust
$500,000 Estate

The "Give it Twice" trust plan is popular with some people. This means you may give it to your family and to a charity too.

You set up a Revocable Living Trust or describe a Testamentary Trust in your Will to be established upon your death. In either case, you continue to own and manage all your assets as long as you live.

Upon your death, your Trustee is instructed to hold and invest the assets of your estate and pay the income out to named members of your family each month.

The trust ends when the family has received an amount equal to the value of the assets at the time of your death. When the trust ends, the assets are distributed to the charity as you specified in your documents.

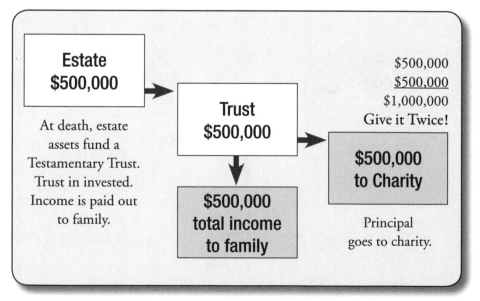

courtesy of W. Robert Daum, CSPG

Charitable Remainder Trust (CRT) Concept

This illustrates the concept of a Charitable Remainder Trust. The Trust provides the donor with income and estate tax benefits; also income for life OR a term of up to 20 years—for the named income beneficiaries (which may be the donor(s) or their children or grandchildren).

When the trust ends, the remainder goes to the charity as the donor specifies in the trust document.

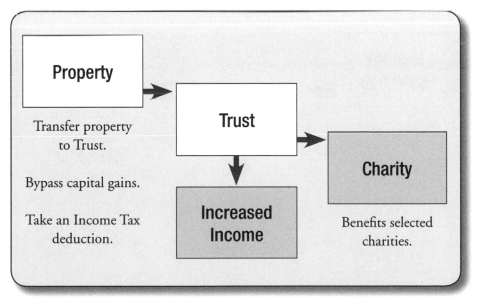

courtesy of W. Robert Daum, CSPG

Income Enhancement Unitrust (Give Three Times)
$350,000 Property

At age 70, John and Mary have an appreciated property valued at $350,000. They would like to enhance their retirement income and quit managing the property.

They are comfortable with equity investments in the stock market. They choose a 7% Income Enhancement Unitrust, which will pay them for life. If the trust investment earns more than the 7% payout, the trust will grow, which means their income will grow—hopefully keeping pace with inflation.

At 70, the income could total over $600,000 during their joint life expectancy of 21.8 years, and will continue to pay them as long as they live.

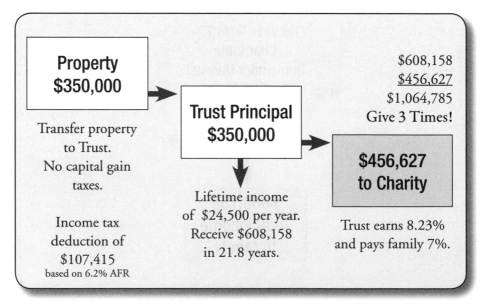

courtesy of W. Robert Daum, CSPG

"Give It Three Times" Trust
$400,000 Property

At age 75, John and Mary are looking forward to helping educate their grandchildren in private colleges or universities. Their goal is to give $10,000 to each of their eight grandchildren. Their income tax bracket is 48% [federal and state], which means they must earn more than $19,000 for each $10,000 gift.

John and Mary have a parcel of land that they pay taxes on and keep the weeds down. They paid $100,000 for it many years ago and today it's worth $400,000.

The range of ages of the grandchildren is such that it will take 20 years to get them all through college, beginning next year. In a 20-year Unitrust, the property is sold with no capital gain tax and they can take an income tax deduction of more than $100,000.

The big bonus is that the income from the trust is taxed in the grandchild's income tax bracket—usually much lower than 48%. The total amount of money to charity at the end of the 20-year trust plus the amount to the eight grandchildren could easily be three times the original value of the property.

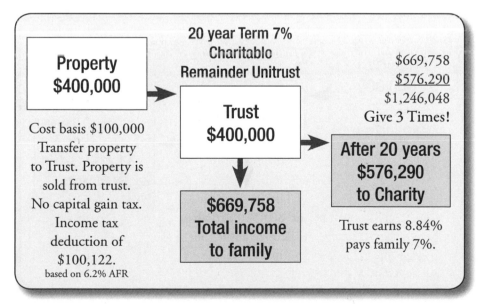

courtesy of W. Robert Daum, CSPG

Living Annuity Trust (Give Three Times)
$1 Million Property

At age 75, John and Mary own property that has increased in value. They don't like the idea of selling it and paying income taxes on the profit (capital gain).

They have a tender heart toward their favorite charity and they want more income to provide for their living expenses.

They are not comfortable with income that depends on equity investments in the stock market. They choose a Living Annuity Trust (a Charitable Trust with the same amount of income every month for as long as they live).

John and Mary keep control of the property even though they give up ownership. They transfer it to the trust, bypass capital gain taxes, and take an income tax deduction. Their bank account receives a direct deposit each month of more than $5,800 on a $1 million trust. During their joint life expectancy of 17.6 years they will receive $1,232,000. Of course, the income continues for as long as they live.

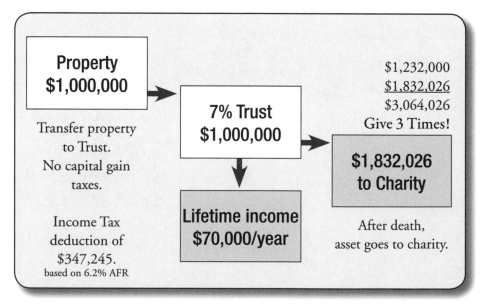

courtesy of W. Robert Daum, CSPG

Deferred Inheritance Unitrust (Give Three Times)
$1 Million IRA

Federal legislation authorizing us to establish Individual Retirement Plans (IRAs) envisioned Americans setting money aside during our working life and spending it during retirement.

And most people with substantial amounts in these financial accounts withdraw only the minimum amount each year because they don't like paying the income taxes on the withdrawals. This means that, for many Americans, IRAs have become an Inheritance Plan rather than a Retirement Plan.

The problem is that children must pay income taxes on the withdrawals, too. If the account is subject to federal and state income taxes and estate taxes, too, the shrinkage may be as much as 80%.

One possible solution is to set up a Deferred Inheritance Unitrust to pay the IRA out to the children in installments for a term of up to 20 years—at which time the trust ends and the remainder goes to the donor's chosen charity where there are no income or estate taxes to be paid. Thus a bad asset, when given outright to the children, becomes a good asset when given to charity.

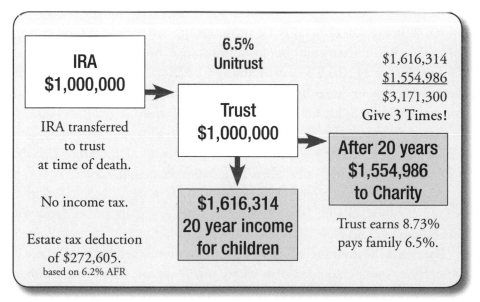

courtesy of W. Robert Daum, CSPG

The preceding gift models are examples of compounding various amounts of money up to three times. Now I am going to show you how to compound various assets or entire estates up to 20 times.

First a little history. In 1968 I was introduced to Barry Kaye, who later became the number one insurance consultant in America. He also got the insurance industry to innovate in many ways. Here are a few.

- In 1963, he was the catalyst for creating the last-to-die survivorship life insurance.
- He was responsible for getting the insurance industry to come up with the one low payment for last-to-die insurance policies.
- He was the first to get the insurance industry to insure individuals for $1 billion. Now it is multiple billions.
- He was the first to see and promote life insurance as an investment, not an expense.
- He found the tax leverage in his combination of "donate and create" technique, using insurance in mathematical ways never used before.
- He came up with dozens of ways to compound individual assets and entire estates up to 20 times or more.

An industry leader, a daily talk show host, and a best-selling author, Barry Kaye has written eight books on insurance, his latest being *You Buy, You Die, It Pays*. He has a dream of raising $1 billion for charity. He and his wife, who are great philanthropists, started by contributing $32 million and compounded it with life insurance. Already it is at the *$500 million mark*!

Barry founded the Barry Kaye School of Finance, Insurance and Economics, and the Barry Kaye Institute of Insurance in Philanthropy, both at Florida Atlantic University, where he lectures on a regular basis.

A noted university bestowed on him an honorary doctoral degree in the humanities for his lifetime achievements in the insurance industry, innovations, and his contributions to mankind.

Barry sees life insurance as money. Money is money regardless of where it comes from. Your heirs and favorite charities will not care whether the money they receive comes from your business, stocks, real estate, or insurance. It is simply money, and it all spends the same after your death.

The best estate planning is to leave the most money for your heirs and favorite charities, **and** the best way to leave the most money is to buy life insurance.

Compound Your Estate with Life Insurance

Did you know that at age 60 you could purchase a $3 million Last-to-Die life insurance policy for one payment of $100,000, all based on your life expectancy? Even up to age 75, you can purchase a $2 million policy or more for the same $100,000. If you borrowed the $100,000, you would pay only $3,000 interest per year.

In this manner, a $500,000 loan could possibly create up to $15 million for your family and charity at a net cost of only $15,000 yearly interest.

$15 million for $15,000 per year!

Here are a few other life insurance ideas:

$ Give to charity, plus a substantial amount for your family, all at no cost.

$ Your Social Security could be worth up to $2 million.

$ Effectively increase your IRA from $1 million up to $20 million.

$ Are you paying too much for your life insurance?
You may be able to double the value of your existing life insurance policy without increasing your premium.

You do not have to die for life insurance to pay off for you.

> *You Buy, You Die, It Pays*
> *You Buy, You Live, It Pays*

What I have given you is just the tip of the iceberg for possibilities on how to compound a specific asset or your entire estate so that you have gigantically more money to leave your family or favorite charity, and all at no or very little expense to you. This is accomplished with low-cost insurance from some of the best insurance companies in the industry.

In summary, purchasing life insurance further diversifies your portfolio. This allows you to look at insurance as simply another investment; it also can help you become a philanthropist and enable you to make money while giving money away.

Only Life Insurance Can...

$ Eliminate death taxes.

$ Create your own charitable foundation.

$ Create trustee income in perpetuity for your children, grandchildren, and great-grandchildren.

$ Create the most money for your family and favorite charity.

Resources

Insurance Information

Alan Kaye Insurance Agency, Inc., 800-662-5433

Barry Kaye, 800-343-7424

- free insurance evaluation
- free IRA/pension analysis
- compound your assets

Annuity Models

W. Robert Daum, CSPG

508-259-3847

rdaum1@verizon.net

Arkad was rich and generous.
Be like Arkad!

Appendix

Have $10 Million on Your 20th Wedding Anniversary

So 20 years after your wedding you are a multimillionaire! This is the miracle of compound interest. You can now choose to "retire" wealthy while young.

	20 YEARS	30 YEARS	40 YEARS
WEDDING SAVINGS	$245,498	$993,176	$4,017,953
REDUCE INCOME TAX	$1,104,470	$4,687,096	$19,180,817
ELIMINATE INTEREST	$1,281,185	$5,437,031	$22,249,748
SALARY #2	$1,851,974	$7,492,268	$30,310,402
401(K)	$1,889,888	$8,776,530	$39,496,576
INCOME TAX REFUND	$302,382	$1,404,244	$6,319,452
INTEREST-ONLY MORTGAGE			
TAX SAVINGS	$942,481	$3,999,655	$16,367,631
LOWER PAYMENT	$757,977	$3,504,910	$15,701,878
$25,000 CUSHION	$409,163	$1,655,294	$6,696,588
TOTAL	$8,785,018	$37,950,204	$160,341,045

Remember, I said you would be worth $10 million 20 years from your wedding date. The other $1.23 million will come from the significant financial solutions and options given in the rest of the book. Choose two or three from Chapter 11 that are best for you and your family. And consider investing in a second 401(k).

Your Children's Investments

Young Child Amount Invested	Total $ Invested	Principal & Interest at age 22	Principal & Interest at age 45
$500 one time at birth, BABY SHOWER	$500	$10,822	$269,385
$600/yr (age 1-4) TOY MONEY-GRANDPARENTS AVERAGE MONEY SPENT ON TOYS EACH YEAR	$2,400	$42,644	$1,061,208
$800/yr (age 1-5) 100% CHILD'S CASH GIFTS	$4,000	$66,752	$1,661,558
$1,000/yr (age 6-11) 75% CASH GIFTS, HIRE CHILD	$6,000	$46,836	$1,165,807
$4,000/yr (age 12-18) CHILD'S ROTH IRA	$28,000	$89,037	$2,216,252
$4,000/yr (age 15-18) CHILD'S EXTRA WAGES WAGES BEYOND ROTH IRA AND 75% CASH GIFTS	$16,000	$40,175	$1,000,006
$3,000/yr (age 19-22) CASH GIFTS, EXTRA WAGES DURING FOUR YEARS OF COLLEGE	$12,000	$17,227	$428,805
Investment Results	**$68,900**	**$313,493**	**$6,637,214**

Young Adult Amount Invested	Total $ Invested	Principal & Interest at age 45
$8,000/yr (age 23-25) AFTER GRADUATION TO WEDDING	$24,000	$522,862
$15,000 Wedding Savings ASSUMES YOU MARRY AT 25	$15,000	$245,498
$9,375/yr Reduce Income Taxes AGE 25-45 (20 yrs)	$187,500	$1,104,470
$10,875/yr Interest not paid to others (20 yrs)	$217,500	$1,281,185
$26,000/yr Second Salary (6 yrs)	$156,000	$1,851,974
$100,000 from Interest-only Home Mortgage (20 yrs) LOW-END AVERAGE, PER YEAR	$0	$2,000,000
401(k) $1,250 per month (20 yrs) EMPLOYEE AND EMPLOYER CONTRIBUTION	$300,000	$1,889,888
Invest $100 twice monthly instead of $2,400 once a year from Income Tax Refund (20 yrs)	$48,000	$302,382
Investment Results	**$948,000**	**$9,198,259**

Principal and Interest at age 45	**$15,835,473**

Income Streams

INCOME STREAMS	Total	10% Annual Return	15% Annual Return	Refer to pg #
NOW				
$25,000 Cash Cushion FOR EMERGENCIES HAVE A HOME EQUITY LINE OF CREDIT	$25,000	$2,500	$3,750	112
Tax-free Income from sale OF APPRECIATED HOME (IF MARRIED)	$500,000	$50,000	$75,000	85
TOTAL Yearly Income		**$52,500**	**$78,750**	
COMPOUNDED for 20 years				
401(k) $1,250 per month EMPLOYEE AND EMPLOYER CONTRIBUTION	$1,889,888	$188,988	$283,483	52
Reduced Income Taxes	$1,104,470	$110,447	$165,670	50
Interest-only home mortgage TAX SAVINGS ($8,000/YR) LOWER PAYMENT ($500/MO)	$942,481 $757,977	$94,248 $75,797	$141,372 $113,696	80/82 80/82
Creampuff used car versus new	$489,653	$48,965	$73,447	106
High school prom savings ($1,000)	$8,138	$813	$1,220	118
Income Tax Refund INVESTED/COMPOUNDED SEMIMONTHLY	$302,382	$30,238	$45,357	55/56
$200 saved per month INVESTED/COMPOUNDED ANNUALLY	$265,415	$26,541	$39,812	26
Invest twice monthly versus annually (FREE MONEY) ($200/MO VS $2,400/YR)	$36,967	$3,696	$5,545	52/53
TOTAL Yearly Income		**$579,733**	**$869,602**	
COMPOUNDED beginning at Birth				
Birth to 45	$15,814,289	$1,581,428	$2,372,144	97
TOTAL Yearly Income		**$1,581,428**	**$2,372,144**	

2000 Ways to Lower Living Expenses

Books

- *1001 Ways to Cut Your Expenses* by Jonathan D. Pond
  Get down to business of spending less money.
- *Penny Pinching 101: Live Better for Less and Stay Out of Debt* by Jackie Iglehart
  > Develop money-saving savvy and end money stress forever.
- *Penny Pinching Fifth Edition: How to Lower Your Everyday Expenses Without Lowering Your Standard of Living*
  by Barbara Simmons and Lee Simmons
  > This edition is expanded and updated to include even more penny-pinching tips. It contains lots of useful Web sites and is an essential for anyone interested in saving money.
- *Pinch A Penny Till It Screams. Everything You Wanted To Know About Frugal Survival Skills But Didn't Know Where To Look* by Madeline Clive
  > Live well without spending much.
- *The Complete Tightwad Gazette* by Amy Dacyczn
  > This book contains hundreds of ideas to lower costs and how to be frugal without feeling deprived.

AAA Important

- Remember, a dollar **saved** is **equal** to $1.65 **earned**.
- Reduce taxes to save and build wealth rapidly.
- Interest paid for credit is the second-largest waste of money **except interest for investments**. Instead of making others millionaires, use that money to invest for yourself. Use a credit card only if you have the cash to back it up and receive 145% more for your money.

Clothing

- Purchase at end-of-season, on sale. Example: $119 designer garment for $15.88.
- $150 brand name sneakers are absurd.
- Many times designer clothing is made in the same sweatshops as other clothes, only with a different label.

Education

See Chapter 10

- Pay tuition on time, avoid paying interest.
- Teach children to be independent at a very early age, to have part-time jobs.
- Create setting so children can earn most or all tuition from third grade on, except for graduate and professional degrees.
- Parents and/or grandparents could invest $10,000 per child at birth to help with college tuition.
- College money help, free scholarship search, free college finance calculators
  - For students
    - 800-891-1410
    - collegeanswer.com
  - For parents
    - 800-891-1410
    - parentanswer.com
- Information on consolidating student loans
  - 800-448-3533
- More info on student loan consolidation
  - loanconsolidation.ed.gov
  - 800-5577392
- Free scholarship search
  - xap.com
  - collegeboard.com
  - princetonreview.com
  - fastweb.com
  - srnexpress.com/index.cfm

- Free financial aid
    This Web site created by a man who funded his schooling
    without any financial help from his parents.
        finaid.org

Entertainment

- Use library books, videos, DVDs—you already pay for these
  with your taxes.
- Videos, CDs, and DVDs—exchange or barter with friends
  or buy at yard sales.
- Sell your CDs
        CashForCDs.com
- Music and books up to 90% off
        800-395-2665 for a catalog
        salebooks.com

Food

- Almost 25% of all food purchases are thrown out.
- Start with small servings and put only food on your plate
  that you will eat. **It costs $3 to replace $1 of wasted food.**
- Purchase in bulk from wholesalers or discount stores.
- Use a freezer and rotate the food.
- Minimize or eliminate purchase of junk food. Cost is 12 to
  100 times more than whole food.
- Minimize purchase and use of ready-made meals.
- Vegetarian diet is less expensive and exceedingly better for
  you.
- Reduce cost of eating out by one-half.
- Buy on sale and stock up. Very high return on investment.
- Save and use coupons. If you are organized, you can make
  $25-$50 hour.
- Read labels and buy the best nutrition for your food dollar.
- Join a local food co-op.
- Drink water instead of soda pop, which is expensive, has no
  food value, and is harmful to your teeth and body.

- *Weimar Institute's NEWSTART® Lifestyle Cookbook: More Than 260 Heart-Healthy Recipes Featuring Whole Plant Foods* by Frances Piper de Vries, Sally J. Christensen
  Newstart stands for the eight elements that give you health, vigor, and healing: Nutrition, Exercise, Water, Sunshine, Temperance, Air, Rest, and Trust in Divine Power. Full of delicious and nutritious recipes that can make a meaningful difference in your life, the Newstart Lifestyle Cookbook is more than a diet plan—it's a new way to live. To order, 530-637-4111.

Gift Giving

Is a habit and should be discontinued in most cases. How do you know what color, size, design, or how many of the same items the person already has? One newlywed couple spent a full week returning more than 150 duplicate gifts. If you must give, give a card and a check. This saves time and wear-and-tear on you, your family, and your car.

What about the need to be generous? Suze Orman said recently, "True generousity is when it is a gift to the person and to yourself. Giving a gift which puts you in credit card debt is not generous." True giving is when it empowers both the giver and the receiver. Be empowered!

Household Help

If you hire household help and stay below $1,000 in any given quarter or $1,500 a year per person, you will save tax withholding and Social Security. And workers' Comp insurance is required for any amount, so check with your homeowner insurance policy before purchasing, because you may be covered already.

Home

- Purchase a low-maintenance, realistic-size home if the house payment is close to the rent cost.
- If you cannot handle an interest-only mortgage, use a 15-year mortgage and pay off as rapidly as possible.

- For all major repairs and remodeling, write specifications, then get multiple bids.
- Refinance when appropriate for lower interest and lower payments to have more money to invest.

Household Appliances and Other Purchases

- Write specifications first.
- Check *Consumer Reports* magazine.
- Purchase most energy-efficient appliances available.
- Get competitive bids.
- At the end, negotiate a lower price still and/or free delivery and installation.
- Pay cash to avoid interest.

Insurance

- Write your auto insurance specifications and get several bids. Prices can vary up to $3,000 per year for two autos.
- Ask for non-smoking and non-drinking policies and all other discounts applicable.
- Combine all insurance with one company where possible for maximum discounts.
- If your life insurance is older than three years, chances are you are paying too much.
- For most life insurance needs, purchase only term insurance.

Medical

- Lower your medical cost gigantically by ordering a set of eight Newstart "Rainbow" booklets for $1.98 on "Eight Natural Physicians" from: Weimar Institute, Catalog Sales Department, Box 486, Weimar, CA 95736. This is the best medical investment you will ever make.
- Practice healthy lifestyle medicine.
- Use larger insurance deductions.

- Affordable medications
    Eldercare Locator
    800-677-1116
    eldercare.gov
    Veterans Administration
    877-222-8387
    va.gov
- Free guidance for consumers on prescription medicines
    CRBestBuyDrugs.org

Stocks

- 70% reduction in commission or more by using discount broker such as Charles Schwab, 800-435-4000. Morgan Stanley Dean Witter in person or on the Internet is least expensive.
- Save paying brokerage fees. Call Horizon Publishing Company, 800-233-5922 on 1,100 companies that sell their stock directly to you, at no cost, and yes, some with a 3% to 5% discount! Also list Dividends Reinvestment Plans (DRIPs).

Utilities

- Electricity, Gas, Water
    Many city-owned utilities will come to your home and do a total energy review at no cost lower your cost 25%.

Telephone

- Write specifications first, then call and get bids. Remember to compare apples with apples.
- With new laws, competition is far greater: 25% to 40% reduction is common.
- Purchase your telephone. Almost 15 million people, mostly elderly, still lease and waste money needlessly each month.
- Generally lower prices can be had by one provider for telephone, Internet, and cable.
- Explore low- or no-cost long distance Internet calling.

Transportation

Vehicles are used to go from point A to B. Your automobile should not be an ego trip. Don't try to keep up with the Joneses because they may be almost bankrupt.

- Purchase quality, one-owner, low-mileage, used cars from individuals you know and trust. Save approximately $4,000 per year.
- Avoid leases and car payments.
- See if you can get by with one car.
- Purchase a car that uses 87 octane and save $1,500 a car. **$1,500 invested yearly @ 15% = $3,068,931 in 40 years**
- Change your own oil and filters if you have time.
- Wash your own car—saves you time and money ($300 a year).
- Save money on auto repairs
  Check the recall list for ones you might have missed
  888-372-4236
  nhtsa.gov

Travel

- Earn a free trip when you sell your house.
  866-502-9273
  awardsformortgageandrealestate.com
- Free flights
  If your schedule permits, volunteer your seat for an overbooked flight. Most airlines give a free travel voucher that you could use for your vacation.
- Free things to do and see
  This site lists free places to visit in Europe and U.S.
  freetodo.net

Additional Ways

- Avoid "malling."
- Forget trying to impress with your possessions.
- Check all statements prior to paying. The average family has double billing or mistakes equaling $1,000 a year.
- Federal Citizen Information Center.
    - Free publications on lots of topics.
    - 888-8-PUEBLO (888-878-3256)
    - pueblo.gsa.gov/
- Join the National Do Not Call Registry
    - 888-382-1222 (from number you wish to register)
    - DoNotCall.gov
- Become a mystery shopper
    - mysteryshop.org/shoppers/info.php

2000 Ways to Lower Income Taxes

According to Congress and the IRS, you are legally entitled to pay the least tax possible. There are many new deductions in the past three tax law changes. See your tax attorney.

Books
- *422 Tax Deductions: For Businesses and Self-Employed Individuals* by Bernard B. Kamoroff, CPA
- *How to Pay Zero Taxes, 2006 Edition*, 23rd Edition by Jeff A. Schnepper
  "Your guide to every tax break the IRS allows. Hundreds of tips and techniques to preserve your income through exclusions, credits, deductions, shelters, smart investments and more."
- *Make Your Life Tax Deductible: Easy Techniques to Reduce Your Taxes and Start Building Wealth Immediately* by David Meier
  Features hundreds of deductions to lower your taxes today.
- *Your Income Tax 2007* by J. K. Lasser
  Rated number one tax reduction book in U.S. with more than 1,000 ways to lower taxes. Updated each year.

Newsletters
- *106 Tax Tips for Older Americans*
  800-829-1040, publication #554
  irs.gov
- *Tax Hotline*
  800-288-1051
  bottomlinesecrets.com/blpnet/offers/subth.html?sid=hplogo
- *Retirement Watch*
  800-552-1152
  Written by Robert C. Carlson, an attorney and CPA who specializes in tax law.

Children

- Dependent care tax credit
- Shift income to children where and when legal. Check with your CPA or your estate planning attorney.
- Report your children's investment income on their tax return, not yours.
- Maximize IRA and/or Roth IRAs for your children age 7 and older.
- Employ your immediate family members, age 7 and up.
- Interest on student loans
- IRS-approved ways to pay all or part of college expenses and be tax deductible:

  ~ Business owners have it easy. Simply put the student-to-be on the company's payroll and direct the salary into a college fund. The salary is deductible to the business. If business is unincorporated and the youth is under 18, Social Security is avoided also.

  ~ Install your child as a board director in your corporation and pay him or her.

  ~ Save money and teach responsibility. Buy rental property near the college campus and hire your child to manage the property on a salary or percentage basis. Your child would have the free manager's apartment. If more than one bedroom, he could rent one out.

Death Taxes—Eliminate or Reduce

Death tax is a voluntary tax. And 70% of adults have not taken the time to properly plan their estate. They pay tens of billions of dollars in needless taxes each year.

- Death taxes are levied by the federal and many state governments.
- Use a living trust and avoid probate court for your estate.
- There are dozens of ways to eliminate or greatly reduce your death taxes. Talk to your CPA or tax attorney.
- Life insurance to pay death taxes is one option.

- Remove your life insurance from your estate.
- Remove appreciating assets from your estate. Talk to your tax attorney or CPA.
- Eliminate all or most death taxes while multiplying your estate up to 15 times at no or very little cost.
Barry Kaye and Associates, 800-662-5433
- You can lower your current income tax, avoid capital gains tax, maintain or increase your annual income for life, and give your children and your favorite charity large sums of money. Talk to your estate planning attorney.
- Retirement plan assets are the most costly to transfer to heirs at death, and the least costly to transfer to a charity. To heirs the plan loses 70%–80% of the value, whereas you get 100% deduction to charity. Give heirs your other assets.

Employment
- An increased expense account is better than an increase in salary in many cases.
- Don't overpay taxes. Most people do so needlessly.
- If you are of the 80% of all taxpayers who received an average $2,500 tax refund this year, then go to your human resources department tomorrow and increase your dependents on a new W-4 form. Increase your take-home pay on your next paycheck and invest immediately.

Give It Away
- $12,000 (cash, stocks, property) can be given each *year* by a single person or $24,000 for a married couple to any number of people without any tax consequences to either party.
  The tax-free limit is waived when you pay someone's medical or school tuition bills, provided you pay the bills directly to the institutions.
- Donate your old car to charity and deduct.
- Contributions give a nice tax deduction.

- Clean out your garage, attic, and basement. Donate clothing, furniture, etc., to charity. Get a receipt and deduct fair market value.
- Smart charity giving that pays you back. Multiply your estate at least 10 times (gift annuities, pooled income funds, and charitable remainder trusts) all tax-free to your retirement, heirs, and charity. Barry Kaye and Associates 800-662-5433.

Home/Real Estate

- For those who qualify, get an interest-only home mortgage and have up to $8,000 per year in lower income taxes. See Chapter 9 for details.
- Deduct seller's paid points as prepaid interest on home sales.
- Deduct mortgage interest.
- Deduct the interest on home equity loans.
- Deduct home property taxes.
- The greatest tax reduction in IRS history is on home sale profits—$250,000 if single and $500,000 if married. If you plan to sell your appreciated home soon, remember, these amounts are 100% tax-free. And you can repeat this every two years if you have great appreciation and like to move.
- Deduct interest on second home.
- Deduct rental property depreciation.
- You can rent real estate to family members. Congress recently changed the rules. The IRS must respect inter-family rentals.
- Give your home to heirs in your living trust.

Investments

- Investment interest paid
- Deduct investment losses
- Tax-preferred securities
- Tax-exempt bonds
- Gas and oil partnership
    Example $20,000 is typical for one unit. In the first year

you can deduct 89% from your taxes, plus 25% income tax deduction on every monthly check you receive. This is a great way to lower income taxes and receive a stream of income for years from your portion of the gas and oil sales.

- Tax-deferred investments
  Invest in quality individual stocks with automatic dividend reinvestment and hold if good investments.
- Deduct your investment expenses:
  ~ Investment counsel
  ~ Subscriptions, books, magazines, newsletters, newspapers, and cable television for business news

  ~ Telephone calls and cellular calls
  ~ Office expenses - clerical, postage, financial, computer

  ~ Tax, legal, and accounting including estate planning
  ~ Custodial fees, account service fees, safe deposit box
  ~ All fees and expenses maintaining an IRA
  ~ Home computer depreciation
  ~ Travel expenses involving investing
  ~ Entertainment, meals, and gifts for tax advisors, brokers
  ~ Reasonable costs to attend an annual stockholders meeting in which you have investments
- Use carry-overs - capital losses, investment interest, unused passive losses, charitable contributions.

Own Your Own Business

- Self-employed individual, working out of your home, have more legal tax deductions than any other trade, skill, or profession. You may deduct more expenses, reduce your income tax, and have more money to invest.
- Be tax-wise when selling your business. See a tax attorney.
- Pay your children a salary to help in your office or home

business beginning at age 7.
- Pay each child $12,500 annually from cottage industry or family business—100% tax deductible.
- Home office expenses.
- Business use of your home.
  Publication #587 from IRS free, 800-829-3676, irs.gov
- Deduct mileage for business, charity and volunteering, medical, and employee moving. 800-829-3676, irs.gov
- Private airplane is a deductible expense if you use for business.
- Classify workers as independent contractors legally. IRS publication 15-A. 800-829-3676, irs.gov

Pension Plans
- A very important way to reduce income tax is your pension plans. You notice this is plural. Max out as many as allowed.
- All states are now barred from taxing pensions of non-residents.
- 401(k)—If your employer has a 401(k) plan, you can deduct from payroll taxes $15,000 or $20,000 if age 50 or older. This is the amount up to 2009.
- 401(k) employer's maximum contribution
- 401(k) contributions: Employers must deposit employee contribution into plan no later than 15 business days after the month the money is collected.
- Some highly compensated employees may be able to increase their annual 401(k) contribution.
- New 401(k) benefit: retirees with money in a former employer's 401(k) must be offered a broader range of investment choices. Formerly some allowed only low-yield money market accounts.
- Smart 401(k) investing: Couples unable to fully fund both retirement plans should concentrate on maximizing contributions to the better one. Focus on plan at companies that make contributions, where you intend to stay long

enough to keep its contributions when you leave, and have wide range of investment options.

- Best **free** pension pocket guide. Pioneer's Retirement Plans 800-622-0176. New, updated issue available every February.
- All other possible pension plans.
- About 25% of employees contribute less than what is allowed by IRS.
  - ~ 50% take too conservative approach to investing.
  - ~ 20% borrow from 401(k), a NO NO!
  - ~ 50% spend half of their balance when they leave the companies, another NO NO!

  A typical retirement now stretches 20 to 50 years.
- Solo 401(k) for self-employed. Deduct up to $44,000 for husband and $44,000 for wife per year tax-free. And with a defined benefit plan, you are allowed $180,000.
- 403(b) for employees of nonprofits such as schools, hospitals, and other tax-exempt 501(c)(3) organizations can also deduct $15,000 per year or $20,000 if 50 and older. Good to at least 2009.
- Simple IRA for employers with 100 or fewer employees. Employees can deduct $10,500 per year, $13,000 if age 50 and older.
- Cash-rich, high-income sole proprietorships and S-company owners who are 50 and older can stash away as much as $175,000 a year for themselves. Source: *The Kiplinger Letter*, April 26, 2006.
- SEP— for sole proprietors, partnerships, corporations, nonprofit, and government entities, contribution limit is 25% of pay (20% for self-employed) up to $45,000 per year.
- Roth IRA— income limit $114,000 for single tax returns and $166,000 joint tax returns. Annual contribution is $4,000 for each working individual. Additional $1,000 age 50 or above. No tax deduction allowed. The amount goes up to $5,000 plus $1,000 for age 50 and older applies to 2009.
- Roth IRA for you.

- Roth IRA for your spouse.
- Traditional IRA—Annual contribution is $4,000 for each working individual. An additional $1,000 if 50 and older. If you participate in an employer's tax-deductible pension plan, the IRA is not tax-deductible.
- Tax-exempt organizations are now able to establish 403(b) plans.
- Wait to age 59 ½ to withdraw from many retirement plans so that you don't pay a penalty, i.e., 50% tax on lump sum 401(k) distributions in most cases.
- 412(i) is a simple defined benefit plan. If you are age 40 or older and have a small business or profession:
    ~ Large annual tax deductions (up to $300,000)
    ~ Plan benefits fully guaranteed
    ~ No investment risk, safety of principal
    ~ Plan contributions are fully tax-deductible
    ~ Plan assets grow tax-free
    ~ Plan assets are protected from judgment creditors
    ~ Eligible for IRA rollover
    ~ Lower administration fees
    ~ Approved in writing by IRS
    ~ Ideal for doctors, dentist, small-business owners, and self-employed
    For more information
    Guardian Life Insurance Company of America
        847-564-0123
    John Koresko, Tax Attorney and CPA
        610-992-2200

Just a few added notes regarding pension plans. Whichever category you fit in, pension plans are at the top of the list in reducing your income taxes every pay period and investing immediately for yourself.

Travel

- Plan vacations around business-related conventions and seminars.
- Volunteers can deduct transportation, food, and lodging.

Veterans

- *Federal Benefits for Veterans and Dependents*
  For veterans, updated yearly
  www1.va.gov/OPA/vadocs/current_benefits.asp

Keys for 401(k) and 403(b) Investing
Start young
Take investment risks early
Leave the money alone
Invest the maximum

Contributions are tax-deductible
investment proceeds tax-deferred

Financial Information That Children Should Know

The following guidelines were adapted from the National Council for Economic Education's voluntary economics standards.

By Grade 4, your child should be able to

- Describe the difference between needs and wants.
- Describe the costs and benefits of a choice.
- Construct a simple budget for an allowance (including money to spend, save, and charitable donations).

By Grade 8, your child should be able to

- Explain compound interest and why it is important to begin investing early.
- Explain inflation's effect on prices.
- Construct a family budget (including money for bills, donations, and saving for multiple goals, such as vacation, college, and retirement).

By Grade 12, your child should be able to

- Explain how credit card interest rates work and the dangers of carrying too much debt.
- Explain inflation's effect on savings.
- Explain how the stock market works.
- Write checks and balance a checkbook.
- Find and compare interest rates charged by local lenders on various types of loans.

In Search of Good Advice
Questions to Ask a Financial Advisor

Vital Questions
- How much experience have you had?
- How much education have you had and in what fields?
- What certification do you have?
- Do you specialize in types of clients or services?
- What is your investment philosophy?
- Will you provide me with an individualized financial plan?
- Will this plan be written? How extensive will it be?
- How often do you review these plans with your clients?
- To what extent will you develop an investment portfolio for me?
- How are fees calculated?
- How much can I expect to pay for your services?
- What do you expect from me in our relationship?
- If our relationship doesn't work out, how would we end it?
- Can you supply references from clients and professionals you work with?
- Have you ever been disciplined by a regulatory agency?

Additional Questions
- Can you describe your typical client?
- What kinds of communications, such as account statements or newsletter, can I expect from you?
- To what extent would your assistants handle client matters?
- How do you keep up on developments in the field?
- Do you recommend specific products, or do you generally describe how investment should be allocated?
- How do you research the products you recommend?
- Through what affiliations (such as broker-dealer or insurance company) do you sell financial products?

8 Important Documents to Prepare Now

Most estate planning attorneys can prepare these documents when they prepare your will and living trust. If you do these yourself, forms are available at nolo.com.

- **Financial Inventory (yearly)**
  List all assets, liabilities, and net worth. Include names, addresses, all account numbers, names of physicians, CPA, and estate attorney, etc.

  Remember, in California alone, $500 million of assets are unclaimed each year, with the state getting the money.

- **Will**
  State your choices of how your estate will be divided and your children cared for.

- **Living Trust**
  It's for management of assets; assigns distribution of property to occur prior to or at death; avoids probate, which lowers taxes and costs.

- **Durable Financial Power of Attorney**
  Authorize a trusted person to make financial decisions on your behalf if you become incapacitated.

- **A Living Will** (advance medical directive)
  States your desires for life-prolonging medical care in terminal conditions if you are unable to communicate your wishes.

- **Health Care Durable Power of Attorney**
  Authorizes someone to make your health care decisions if
  you are unable (other than life-death matters).

- **Organ and Tissue Donor Arrangements**
  Each organ and tissue donor saves or improves the lives of as
  many as 50 people.
  Contact the closest organ procurement center
      800-989-9455
      organdonor.gov/organizations/organ_procurement.htm
  For a donor card
      organdonor.gov/signup1.html

- **Burial Instructions**
  Include topics such as body donation to medical school for
  research, cremation, regular burial, cemetery, and all the
  details for your funeral or memorial service. Call a local
  funeral home for a free planning guide.

People are divided into three groups

Those who MAKE things happen
Those who WATCH things happen
Those who WONDER what happened

Which group do you choose to be in?

I hope that you are in the first group and make your estate happen
today—for you, your family, and your favorite charities.

Disclaimer

The purpose of all examples in this book is to encourage you to begin investing. The calculations are from interactive online calculators and are not intended to provide investment advice. Taxes and inflation were not considered for obvious reasons.

This book is designed to provide accurate and authoritative information in regard to the subject matter covered. Factual material has been obtained from sources believed to be reliable, and is not guaranteed. All examples are for illustrative purposes only and are not to be construed as recommendations, advice, or tax counsel. The author and publisher are not engaged in rendering legal, accounting, or other professional financial service. If legal or other expert assistance is required, the author and publisher strongly recommend that the reader contact his or her own professional advisors.

Past performance should not be taken as being representative of future results. Anything tax-related should be discussed with your accountant before it is used for tax purposes. All information provided in this book is for informational purposes only.

Every effort has been made to make this book as complete and accurate as possible. And there may be mistakes, both typographical and in content. Therefore, this text should be used only as a general guide and not as the ultimate source of financial information. Furthermore, this book contains information that is current only up to the printing date.

The author and SG&A Productions shall have neither liability nor responsibility to any person or entity with respect to any loss or damage caused, or alleged to have been caused, directly or indirectly, by the information contained in this book.

About the Author

Having started his first business at age 11, Paul S. Damazo has extensive experience in building many profitable, successful businesses. His latest, begun with one person, quickly grew to more than 2,500 employees within five years.

In less than 14 months following college graduation, he completed a full-time dietetic internship and obtained a master's degree in administrative dietetics with a 3.9 GPA from Florida State University. Later he became a registered industrial engineer, a skill that he used extensively in his businesses.

For 21 years, he taught part-time in the graduate schools of Loma Linda University and UCLA, both in Southern California.

And his passion for finance and investing became his hallmark. Paul started investing at the age of 15. For 50 years his proven investment strategies have earned him an annual average return of 15% or more.

He says his biggest financial mistake was to give $11 million to various charities by age 45. Due to the "miracle" of compounding interest, had he kept that money invested instead of giving it away, he would have been able to contribute $11 million **each** to 273 charitable organizations today.

Mr. Damazo is more than an accomplished businessman and generous philanthropist. He is a proven inspirer. He shows how almost anyone can become a millionaire and even a multimillionaire if he or she chooses to.

For the past 20 years, he has helped untold numbers of people all across the country with his seminars on Wealth Creation and Wealth Preservation. He has a passion for helping people, especially young people, to have a more peaceful, happy life by making better financial decisions.

He firmly believes:

> *Wealth is not a matter of chance,*
> *it's a matter of choice—your choice.*

Choose to Become Wealthy While Young!